Three More Screenplays

by Greg Dorchak

Other books by Greg Dorchak:

Three Screenplays by Greg Dorchak
Of Pigs and Meteorites
Good Shit To Know About Being A Film Actor
How To Pull A Movie Out Of Your Ass
Who Took My Crayons?!
Where Monsters Go When You Grow Up

Three More Screenplays

by Greg Dorchak

Gold Dust

Kopy Kings

Comics and Robbers

Austin, Texas

Screenplays, by their nature,
are both short stories and novels.
One... on the page,
the other... in the mind.

For my wife Carmen,
who worked so hard to
get Kopy Kings made.

Contents

Three More Screenplays
by Greg Dorchak

GOLD DUST

I think this is the second screenplay I ever wrote, and it will hold a special place in my heart as well, mostly because of what it represents to me.

When our first child was born, I was working graveyard shift at a print shop, and would frequently work second shift, getting home around 11pm. My wife would hand off the baby to me, and I would lay on the couch with that bundle of joy on my chest to help her sleep. She had colic the first several months of her life, then went right into teething – no sleep for anyone to say the least. So I'd find the "oldies" movie channel on TV and just lay there watching the classics till 8am.

One week they had a "Buddy Road Picture" theme, and they played all the old Bob Hope/Bing Crosby movies. I bought a stack of VHS tapes and taped them all, cutting out the commercials, and watched them over and over.

I really loved those Road Pictures, and so when I started writing screenplays I wanted to write my own as homages. The places I had my down-on-their-luck con men going were mythical places: El Dorado, Shangri-La, Atlantis.

This story started out as *Road to El Dorado*, and my circle of friends really liked it, so I sent it to some screenplay competitions and fellowships. However, a year or so later a movie came out called *Road to El Dorado*, though it was animated and not quite the same story as mine, I was furious. I thought I had lost a good script and story. But then I realized, all I really needed to do was re-group, re-name, and move forward. So I re-named it *Gold Dust*.

Then I had a chance to get it on the radio as a radio play, so I rewrote it for that purpose, and that version walked around for a bit. After the radio station was bought-out, I took the story back to the screenplay version to keep shopping it around.

Eventually, around the time of Covid, some friends and I got together and we made it into an old-timey type radio play, and had it on the air in a few small town stations. It was really quite fun hearing it come to life that way, and I still have hopes that one day it gets made as a movie.

Over the years I had started writing two more scripts, but also was doing comic book art to make them into short-run comics. I lost track of most of that artwork, and I think the scripts may have been lost to time and hard drive crashes and swap-outs – but *Gold Dust* remains and I still dig it, and I hope you do, too.

FADE IN

EXT — 1940'S SMALL TOWN TEXAS — DAY

SAM DONAVAN — 30's, handsome, well-dressed — stands on the ground next to a wooden storefront sidewalk.

Next to him sits a large, wooden box with gears, levers and fasteners on it. The box sits on a step halfway up a set of wooden stairs. Six identical boxes sit in a row on the sidewalk.

Sam gestures to the box to attract attention from passing people.

> SAM
>
> (to himself) This just might be the day, Sam Donavan, this just might be the day. (aloud, to the people) C'mon people, look here, you see this invention? It cuts your workload in half. Honest and for sure, this contraption sitting here before you does all the work your ax can do in less than half the time.

He plays to the crowd that gathers, winking to a few women who stop to listen.

INT — BENEATH THE RAISED SIDEWALK — SAME TIME

HORACE FLETCHER — 30's, goofy, brawny — crawls on his belly, pushing a bundle of firewood ahead of him. He is under the wooden sidewalk Sam is standing on, and we can hear Sam muffled overhead.

EXT — SIDEWALK — SAME TIME

A small gathering of people has assembled in front Sam.

> SAM
>
> Good day, my fine people. My name is
> Sam Donavan and I'm with Chop-O, Inc.
> I'm here today to show you something
> that just may make your life that much
> easier.

He directs their attention with a flourish to the box
with gears and levers.

> Introducing CHOP-O! That amazing
> wood-splitting device that handles the
> back-breaking work of an entire day, in
> less than half that time! That is cor-
> rect! You heard me right — Chop-O, when
> properly operated, takes whole logs —
> up to twenty inches in diameter and 18
> inches in length — and gives back preci-
> sion cut fire wood!

> MAN

How's it do that? It's jest a box.

> SAM

"Just a box"? My good man, this is a
highly technical instrument developed
by Dr. H. Theopolous Fletcher, who, as
a young man in the Oregon Territory,
worked in logging camps and foresaw —
if you'll excuse the pun — the need for
just such a system of changing bulky,
rough-hewn logs into entirely manageable
smaller pieces of firewood. Observe — I
place into Chop-O,

Loudly, for Horace to hear, as he opens the lid.

> an 18 inch pine log,

Drops log in with a thunk.

> I crank this dial to accommodate the
> length, activate the safety feature;
> pull this lever, turn this crank, and
> voila!

He opens the front panel and inside is a pile of
chopped firewood. The crowd "oohs" and "ahs."

                         SAM

          Amazing, isn't it?!

INT — BENEATH SIDEWALK — CONTINUOUS

                      HORACE

          (Mocking) "Amazing, isn't it?" It's
          amazing I let him talk me into this
          crap.

We hear a muffled voice from above

                      SAM VO

          12 inch cedar log.

Horace hustles, checking tags to find a pile of cedar
wood. There is a thunk and he opens the back hatch,
places the cedar wood in, and takes out the log.

EXT — SIDEWALK — CONTINUOUS

Sam opens the front hatch to reveal the split wood

                         SAM

          And Voila! Perfect the first time, every
          time. And now, ladies and gentlemen, the
          offer: I have here six identical Chop-O
          Firewood splitters — each for the stu-
          pendously low low price of twenty-five
          dollars.

                       WOMAN

          That's a lot of money.

                         SAM

          When compared to the time and toil you
          could save, my dear lady, it's no money
          at all — in fact, I am authorized by Dr.
          Fletcher himself at Chop-O headquarters,
          to go as low as twenty dollars during
          this first week of direct sales — thir-
          ty dollars for customized versions for
          shingle makers and spindle turners.

                         MAN

          Wow! Can that thing cut kindling too?

> SAM
>
> Can it cut kindling? (loudly, stomping
> foot) Can it cut kindling?

From inside sidewalk, Horace thumps the box

> SAM
>
> (with a loud cough) Why sure it can! Ob-
> serve, this Ten inch siding board, oops.

He drops it on the sidewalk, it lands with a thunk.

Excuse me folks it's my first day with my new fingers!

The crowd laughs, he bends down to pick it up, and as
the crowd watches, Horace opens the back hatch, drops
in a pile of cut kindling, and feels around for the
board.

The crowd shouts "cheater" and "get them" threats. Sam
looks up at the crowd, follows their gaze to Horace
feeling around inside the box.

> SAM
>
> Oops, forgot to activate the safety
> feature.

The crowd moves in as Sam hurriedly pulls Horace out
through the hole.

> SAM
>
> That wound heal yet, boy?

> HORACE
>
> Which one?

> SAM
>
> Alabama.

> HORACE
>
> Yeah, why?

> SAM
>
> Cause I'd hate it to re-open while these
> fine people give us new ones. Time to go.

They hustle out of the immediate area.

Sam and Horace run down a dirt road with an angry mob
chasing them.

SERIES OF SHOTS

EXT — STREET CORNER — DAY

Sam and Horace on a street of a different town selling bottles of stuff. Horace takes a swig from a marked bottle, then flexes his muscles to show how strong he feels.

People buy bottles, just as a frantic WOMAN shows up with two POLICE OFFICERS in front of her. She points accusingly at Sam and Horace through the cops.

The crowd glares and chases them off.

EXT — ALLEY — NIGHT

Sam and Horace are backed up against a dead-end alley with an angry mob moving in slowly.

EXT — BUSY STREET — DAY

Horace, with bandaged body parts, running a "shell game," he keeps winning.

A MAN becomes angry, grabs his arm. Horace's coat flies open and a huge load of "peas" spill onto sidewalk. Horace smiles weakly and runs.

Sam shakes his head sadly.

EXT — CITY PARK — DAY

In front of a gazebo a sign reads "From far off India, Fletcher the Fakir". Sam plays the crowd as Horace, in boxer shorts, lies down on a bed of nails. The crowd makes astonished faces and points at the sight.

A real FAKIR (in turban and loincloth) enters and starts shouting at Sam and Horace. It becomes apparent that Horace has "borrowed" his bed of nails.

Horace gets to his feet and turns his BACK to us in argument. A sheet of heavy rubber cut out in his outline is attached to his back. Cops break up the conflict.

EXT — BUS STATION — DAY

Sam and Horace hurry onto tour bus, then the bus pulls away from the station. A few seconds later another mob descends on the bus stop and watches as the bus pulls away.

EXT — DESERT — DAY

Bus tools through desert, dust is flying. It is an old tour bus, dirty and worn. Sign in front window of bus reads "Mexico City." The bus passes a road sign and as the dust clears we see the sign reads

"Mexican Border 40 miles."

INT — BUS — following

A mostly Hispanic crowd of hot and tired people occupy the seats. Sam and Horace sit near the back.

> HORACE

> "Let's go on a trip" he says, "See the world" he says, "No" I says, "I want to go back home to Piney Falls" I says, "Let go of me and stop whining" he says.

> SAM

> Oh, c'mon, Junior, a trip south'll do us good this time of year-it's still snowing in Piney Falls.

> HORACE

> What am I, a goose? I can't take a little snow, I gotta head south? What's so great about Mexico anyway, what d'they got? Just a lot of bandits and sand and dust and,

More than half the Mexican men and women turn and glare at Horace.

> HORACE

> Heh heh, and those wonderful bullfights.

> SAM

> That's Spain.

> HORACE

> You're darn right it's a pain. Do you have any idea how long it took to save all that money we had? Then one word from you and pow! We're on the road again and nearly broke!

> SAM

> Now, now, we're not broke.

Horace opens a change purse, dust and moths fly out.

> HORACE

> No, we're not broke, we've got moths

leasing our wallet for a dollar and
some change, and they're behind on
their rent.

                    SAM

Oh come off it, Horace, we needed a
vacation, we've been pushing too hard
for too long, wearin' ourselves out

                  HORACE

"Wearin' ourselves," YOU been wearin'
MY-self out, you have. "Fearless Fletcher the Fire Walker" you make me do.

                    SAM

Ah, The Fire Walker.

He smiles in fond remembrance and he leans back in
his seat.

                  HORACE

Yeah, you rake me over the coals and YOU
rake in the loot.

                    SAM

You're the one who blew all that take
for YOUR foot surgery.

                  HORACE

Well I wouldn't have needed foot surgery if we'd a just painted the coals
red like I wanted instead of usin' real
burning ones. Cripes, who woulda known
the difference?

                    SAM

Well maybe YOU can live with yourself
doing something only half-way, but not
me, son. We used real coals for one
reason, and one reason only: I'd know
the difference. I would, and so would
Aunt Margie.

                  HORACE

Aunt Margie, Sam.

                    SAM

No, Junior,

Sam takes out a pocket watch, opens it and sees a picture of Aunt Margie, who looks a lot like Horace.

                         SAM

          I promised your dear old Aunt Margie
          as I sat there holding her frail,
          wrinkled hand that I'd watch over you
          when she was gone. "Watch over my
          Horace" she said. "Make me proud of him"
          she said. "I will" I said, "Don't let
          him take the low road" she said. And
          then... she left us.

                       HORACE

          Golly. I'm sorry Sam, I didn't mean to
          be selfish.

                         SAM

          No, Junior, you never MEAN to be, but,
          never mind. Just remember next time we
          do "Horace the Hulk, Boulder Catcher,"
          you're doing it for Aunt Margie and me,
          not for YOUR own gain.

Sam puts the watch away, wipes at a tear, and turns to the window.

                       HORACE

          Aw gee, Sam.

Horace hangs his head and whimpers just as the bus lurches to a halt. Sam and Horace look to the front of the bus.

The driver looks into mirror over the back of his seat.

                       DRIVER

          Okay, we got a ten minute stop. You kin
          stretch yer legs and get a snack, don't
          wander off too far.

                       HORACE

          Aw, what're we, babies? "Don't wander
          off," like we're gonna get lost or,

Horace suddenly can't find Sam and panics

          GAAAAHHH! Sam, where are you?

He turns, Sam is standing next to him in the aisle

          Hey, how'd you do that?

                    SAM

      Let's go, Horace. If you're a good boy
      I'll get you a soda.

                  HORACE

      Great. I got this taste in my mouth that
      feels like a New Jersey landfill looks.

                    SAM

      Must be those taco wrappers we had for
      breakfast. Come on, let's go.

EXT — BUS — DAY

We see people as they exit the bus. Sam and Horace
exit, stopping to wait for people ahead of them, some
who give them dirty looks.

                  HORACE

      Speaking of which, when is it my turn to
      eat again?

                    SAM

      What's today?

                  HORACE

      Saturday, why?

                    SAM

      Well, I've got weekends, remember? And
      weekdays with an 'S' in them.

Horace counts on his fingers, is displeased with the
answer he comes up with

                  HORACE

      Hey, that makes every day.

He hurries after Sam

INT — BUS STOP — DAY

Bus riders enter through the dirty glass doors. It is a
small, dusty last-stop-before-end-of-the-line type of
place.

Sam and Horace check out the place just inside doors,
people enter and leave behind them, sun shines in
through windows and glass doors.

Sam spots something to one side and starts in that
direction.

                    SAM

     Well, boy, see what you can dig up over
     there, I'll check over here.

                  HORACE

     Okay, Pop, I'll let you know what I find,
     right after I make a pit stop

Horace starts to head into ladies' room

                    SAM

     Uh, Horace.

                  HORACE

     Hmmm?

Sam indicates the sign on the door, then jerks thumb in
other direction.

                    SAM

     Over there.

Horace looks up at sign, surprised, grins stupidly.

                  HORACE

     Oh, was I, heh heh, honest mistake,

Horace reads sign on door of ladies room.

          "Broom closet," I wanted the little
          boys' room.

Hurries off toward the other restroom.

                    SAM

          Where did your mother and I go wrong?

INT — TICKET COUNTER — DAY

Horace passes the ticket counter where the service
person is discussing something with a customer in
Spanish. He stops to ask a question, stares stupidly at
the two, they stop and look at Horace.

                  CUSTOMER

     (In Spanish) <Excuse me, I'm almost
     finished here?>

                TICKET AGENT

     <One moment, sir, I'll be right with
     you.>

Horace's eyes light up, and he nods stupidly.

                              HORACE

          Ah, Oui! La plume de ma tante est sur la
          table, et la vache est dans le mer.

Agent and customer look at each other, then back at
Horace

                              AGENT

          <You're obviously nuts, go away or I'll
          call the cops.>

He jerks his thumb in the other direction.

                              HORACE

          Oh, it's that way? Thanks a bunch.

He hurries away in the direction given.

          HA. And Sam said that Berlitz German
          course was a waste of time.

The customer looks after Horace.

                              CUSTOMER

          (in Spanish) Pendejo.

Back to ticket agent.

          <Look, I need to get to Dallas by
          tomorrow morning, how do I>

INT — LUNCH COUNTER — SAME TIME

Sam leans on the counter, eyeing food in glass case:
pies, sandwiches, sodas, etc. A WAITRESS, BILLI,
approaches him.

                              BILLI

          What do you need, Sugar?

                              SAM

          Well, I NEED two sandwiches. One corned
          beef, one turkey and peanut butter. Two
          slices of pecan pie, two cups of Joe and
          a bottle of Ginger Ale.

                              BILLI

          Sure honey, comin' up. Was that "turkey
          and peanut butter?"

Starts to get out food onto the counter and prepare it,
pours two cups of coffee.

                    SAM

        Yes, turkey, but, uh,could I get that on
        credit, I, uh,

                    BILLI

        You mean, you don't want to pay for all
        this?

                    SAM

        No, I'd LOVE to pay for it, I just, seem
        to be, caught a tad short at the moment.
        Was kinda hoping to work something out.

He smiles his best smile at her, leans further in on
the counter. The waitress softens up a little.

                    BILLI

        Well, what do you have?

Sam fiddles with his fingers on the countertop.

                    SAM

        Oh, I'll tell you what,

He reads her name tag.

        Billi, you're a real smart looking girl,
        if you can just guess.

A POLICE OFFICER steps up to lunch counter and sits on
a stool, pulls out a paper and reads while he talks.

                    OFFICER

        Hiya Billi, what's good today?

Billi turns from Sam to the officer.

                    BILLI

        Excuse me a second, Sugar. Hey Hank! How
        about I get you a big old slab of Turk's
        meatloaf smothered in mushroom gravy,
        mashed potatoes, corn bread, one 0' my
        famous malts, and a huge wedge of pecan
        pie with whipped cream?

                    HANK

        Oh, sure. But 1 uh, "86" the whipped
        cream, huh, Billi, wife says I need to
        lose some weight!

He turns to Sam, does a half salute.

        Hiya pal, nice day, huh?

Sam turns from Hank, drops a quarter on the counter, takes the cups of coffee, disguises his voice

              SAM

        Yeah, sho' 'nuf.

He quickly shuffles away. Billi turns back to where Sam was standing.

              BILLI

        So what'll it be mister?

She sees he is gone, shrugs and takes the quarter.

        I'll get that loaf, Hank, you just sit
        tight!

Walks back toward kitchen, shouts.

        Turk, number two, Shake it.

INT — BUS STATION — DAY

Horace approaches a men's room door, he reads the door sign.

            HORACE

        Dang, sure are a lot of broom closets in
        this little station.

He turns and looks stupidly around the station for a restroom. MAN 1 rushes past to use the facilities, bumping into Horace.

            MAN #1

        Hey, watchit, Mac, Get outta the way.

            HORACE

        Take it easy there, brother, you can
        sweep up later.

            MAN #1

        What're you, some kinda wise guy?
        Shove off!

He pushes Horace away, and he bumps into a counter where MAN 2 stands.

            MAN #2

        Can I help you?

                    HORACE

     Yeah, where can a guy go to powder his
     nose around here?

The man looks around suspiciously, Horace joins him.

                    MAN #2

     Maybe, you should go.

                    HORACE

     That's the general idea, pal! I been
     sitting on a bus for six hours and I'm
     about three minutes from needing a new
     pair of pants here.

The man grabs Horace by the collar, pulls him down and
close to his face.

                    MAN #2

     No, you ijit! Maybe you should go east
     of town to where the road stops and the
     ROAD begins. He holds the treasure of a
     city long lost -and with his stores of
     gold you'll need never toil again.

He stuffs an old brochure in Horace's hand. Horace
stares at the man, takes the brochure and backs up a
few steps.

                    HORACE

     Look, pal, I just need to use the facil-
     ities. I don't need to solve riddles,
     or, or, think or anything.

                    MAN #2

     GO! Where the road ends! The ROAD
     begins!

A hand touches Horace's shoulder, it is Sam. Horace
jumps.

                    HORACE

     YIIII... I Whoa, Sam, Don't do that.

                    SAM

     Don't what, Boy?

                    HORACE

     Don't spook someone when they're being
     frightened! This guy here already

He jerks a thumb toward the counter, Man #2 is gone.

       Where'd he go?

                    SAM

       Never mind, Junior, let's blow. Your
       uncle's at the lunch counter.

Points back toward Hank

                 HORACE

       Really, Uncle Barnaby? Small world. Hey,
       Unc, Yeesh!

Horace sees the police officer, turns back to Sam.

                   SAM

       By the way, here's your lunch and
       dinner.

Sam hands Horace a cup of coffee.

                 HORACE

       Gee, thanks, Sam, But I thought I didn't
       get anything 'till Monday.

                   SAM

       Ooh, that's right!

Sam takes cup back, downs its contents, hands it back.

                   SAM

       Here, find a receptacle.

                 HORACE

       Okay, lemma find a... why am I looking
       for an octopuses arm?

Hank looks at them, then pulls a flyer out of his
hat. On the flyer are sketches of Sam and Horace with
"REWARD" over them. Hank shoots a glance back to Sam
and Horace, starts to get up.

                   SAM

       Yow! Time to go.

                 HORACE

       Right behind you.

Horace drops the cup on the floor. Sam points down at
the cup as he heads toward door.

                              SAM

          Hey! We don't litter.

                            HORACE

          Oops! Yeah, we don't

Horace bends to pick up the cup, but sees Hank
adjusting his pistol belt.

          I'm no custodian!

He rushes out after Sam.

EXT — BUS — DAY

Sam and Horace quickly board the bus again.

INT — BUS — DAY

                            DRIVER

          Good deal, we just about left without
          you. Take your seats please.

Sam and Horace quickly find their seats and slump down
low.

INT — BUS STATION - DAY

Hank straightens his belt and is ready to pursue Sam
and Horace. Billi appears with pot of coffee.

                            BILLI

          Where Y'all going? Free refills, And you
          ain't had your pecan pie!

                            HANK

          Those guys! They're the. Ooh! Free re-
          fills?!

His eyes light up, he sits and resumes eating.

INT — BUS — DAY

Sam and Horace sit in their seats, dejected.

                            SAM

          We need some cash flow, Junior. I spent
          my last quarter on that coffee.

                            HORACE

          What do you mean, "your" last quarter,
          I'm the only one with any money left.

                    SAM

    You caught me, son, I spent YOUR last
    quarter.

                  HORACE

    How could you, Sam? You said that I
    could keep that for college some day.
    And I didn't even get any coffee.

                    SAM

    There you go again, Boy, only think-
    ing of yourself. What would Aunt Margie
    think of you?

Sam starts to take out the pocket watch.

                  HORACE

    Oh, layoff with Aunt Margie, already Sam.
    I can't handle being broke, hungry and
    guilty all at the same time.

Horace sits and pouts a moment or two. Then, without
turning to Sam.

    So how do we make some dough on this
    horse cart?

                    SAM

    Don't know.

Glances around bus, forming a plan.

    But we'd better come up with something
    quick, we're gonna be in Mexico in under
    an hour.

Horace thinks for a second or two, then lights up.

                  HORACE

    I got it! C'mere, listen, Sam, this
    can't miss.

                    SAM

    Whoa! Hold on there, son. I'm supposed
    to do all of the thinking here.

                  HORACE

    Oh, nonsense, Sam. I can think if
    absolutely necessary, can't I? Now,
    look here, this is a foolproof plan.

He whispers to Sam, who nods and starts to dig around
in their satchel.

EXT — BUS ON ROAD — DAY

The bus comes to a screeching halt. Its doors open and
Sam and Horace are thrown out head-first into sand.
The wind is picking up. Doors slam shut; open again,
satchel is thrown out, doors slam, bus screeches· off
again. Horace and Sam's faces raise slowly out of the
sand. Sam turns to Horace.

                         SAM

          "Foolproof", eh?

                    HORACE

          Well, if it weren't for that one guy
          catching on and knocking me silly, I
          think it would have gone great.

                         SAM

          That "guy's" name was Susan.

                    HORACE

          Yeah, but she was a bruiser. Did you see
          the size of her arms?

Sam gets up, dusting himself off. Horace follows.

                         SAM

          She was nine years old, boy, what's the
          matter with you?

                    HORACE

          Nine years old?!

Shocked, touches his bloody lip.

                    HORACE

          That's child abuse!

Sam looks after the bus which leaves a trail of dust
behind it as it speeds off.

                         SAM

          Looks like we're afoot now.

                    HORACE

          Shouldn't that be "afeet," there's two
          of us.

Sam stares at Horace, then smacks him upside his head.
He walks down the road, Horace picks up the satchel and
follows.

SAM

Let's go, Horace, we've got a long walk
ahead.

HORACE

I thought we were "afoot?"

Sam slaps him again. A second later,

Ouch.

EXT — EDGE OF THE ROAD — LATE AFTERNOON

Horace and Sam's feet are at the edge of the blacktop.
Sand blows around.

SAM

Hmm.

HORACE

What do you mean "Hmm". Where's the
road, Sam? There's no road, Sam, it just
stops, Sam. Where is it? .

SAM Don't know. Must have taken a wrong turn in this
dust, and it's starting to get worse.

HORACE

Whoa, the road stops.

SAM

You just figured that out?

HORACE

Sam, the road stops!

SAM

Oh, we're not gonna have another ugly
incident like with Macy's Santa Claus
are we?

HORACE

No, I know he's not the real one now,
he's just a helper. That guy can't be
everywhere at once, especially in that
part of New York. No, I'm talking about
this.

Horace pulls out the brochure and hands it to Sam,
gesturing wildly at the edge of the road. Sam looks
over the brochure, and hands it back to Horace.

> SAM
>
> We haven't got the time or the money to
> hit tourist traps, Junior. This sand
> is getting pretty bad, head into those
> rocks.

Sam begins to make his way toward a rock formation/cave
with brush around it. Horace follows, still holding the
brochure.

> HORACE
>
> I haven't got rocks in my head, Sam,

Pointing at head.

> There's nothing up there. That guy at
> the bus stop, he gave me this.

> SAM
>
> Not now, boy, let's find us some shelter,
> look! a cave, come on!

They huddle into the small cave and dust themselves off.
Horace sits, leaning on a mound, Sam drops onto the
floor.

> HORACE
>
> Sam, that spooky guy I was talking to at
> the bus stop said it was real, someplace
> called El Torito's or something, it's
> right here, see?! Also said something
> about him having a map to a treasure and
> not needing any foil.

Sam looks disbelieving at Horace. He shakes his head as
if trying to clear it.

> SAM
>
> What are you talking about, Horace? Who
> said what about where?

> HORACE
>
> Read this Sam, it's all here. I'd read
> it to you, but I'm illegitimate.

> SAM
>
> That's illiterate.

                    HORACE

        I do not act like a girl!

Sam takes brochure, reads it over, shaking his head as
he finishes.

                    HORACE

        Well? What do you think? Let's go find
        it, can we Sam? Let's go looking, Sam,
        just like he said, "Road ends, road be-
        gins" he said, "He'd" have a map, he
        said and.

                    SAM

        Settle down, Junior This is a flyer for a
        ghost town. An old tourist trap out in
        the desert, probably isn't even around
        anymore.

Tosses it back at Horace.

        Now lay down, might as well sleep out
        this storm.

Sam stretches out. Horace picks up the brochure slowly,
folds it up and tucks it in his shirt pocket.

                    HORACE

        Aw, gee whiz, Sam, it wouldn't hurt to
        go looking.

                    SAM

        Go to sleep, Horace.

Horace fluffs up the satchel for a pillow and lays down.
He pulls out the brochure again to look at it.

It reads: "Little 'Dorado, the city of Gold!" There is
a picture of old ghost town, "A fortune in gold hidden
within the town for almost a hundred years!"

                    HORACE

        Shoot, Sam's probably right. How real
        can it be if it says "broom closet" on
        the front cover.

He puts brochure away, closes his eyes, opens them
again, turns toward Sam.

        Sing me to sleep Sam.

                              SAM

        No.

                            HORACE

        Oh, come on, Sam, I can't sleep. Sing me
        to sleep.

                              SAM

        No, I'm tired.

                            HORACE

        Okay then, sing yourself to sleep and
        I'll listen in.

Sam throws a rock and hits Horace in the head.

        Thanks, Sam, you're so good to me.

He passes out.

INT — CAVE — DAY

Sunlight fills the small cave. Horace wakes up and looks
over to where Sam was lying the night before. All he
sees is a skeleton, missing some bones.

A scroll of aged paper is in its hand. A tortoise sits
next to it chewing on a prickly cactus.

                            HORACE

        Sam? Sam? Oh my God!

He cradles the skull in his hands.

        "Go south" you said, "Let's see Mexico"
        you said, "No" I said, "There's danger-
        ous animals in the desert" I said, "Get
        off my leg" you said,

Horace looks at the tortoise.

        You, you monster! (sobs hysterical-
        ly) You killed my best friend, my only
        friend in the whole world and ate him!

Waves a hand at tortoise.

        Scat, Shoo! You won't get me, not with-
        out a fight!

Makes a fist and shakes it at tortoise, inadvertently
breaking the skull from the skeleton.

        Ahhh! Sam. What have I done to you?

Sam appears next to Horace and looks at the skeleton
and tortoise.

                         SAM

        What's the problem, boy? You look like
        you've seen a ghost.

                        HORACE

        It's terrible, Sam. This coyote ate you,
        and now I pulled your head off, Yow!

Horace just notices who he's talking to.

                        HORACE

        Sam! Then who's this, and what's that?

Points to shelled reptile.

                         SAM

        Relax, son, it's just a prairie dog or
        something. Say, what's this?

Sam picks the scroll up and opens it. Horace makes a
face at the tortoise.

                        HORACE

        What's it say, what's it say?!

                         SAM

        Easy, Horace.

                        HORACE

        How'd it know my name?

                         SAM

        I said that. (pause) Let me look for a
        minute, will you? Come on out into the
        light, this looks like a map or some-
        thing.

They exit the cave, Horace picks up their satchel and
follows.

                        HORACE

        A MAP? Hey, what that guy told me.

                         SAM

        Yeah, looks like this may be on the
        level after all.

Horace reads over Sam's shoulder, Sam becomes more and
more enthused as he reads on.

>   Horace, this IS a treasure map!
>   HORACE
>
>   No foolin'?
>
>   SAM
>
>   Well, half a treasure map anyway, It's
>   been torn. The actual location is on the
>   other piece.
>
>   HORACE
>
>   That's alright, I can live with half the
>   treasure.
>
>   SAM
>
>   But we can follow this to the little
>   town here, maybe find the other half,
>   then split the whole thing two ways for
>   ourselves!
>
>   HORACE
>
>   Oh. So, so how do we find it, where do we
>   start, how long,
>
>   SAM
>
>   Horace, my boy, looks like we're on our
>   way to your lost city of gold after all.
>
>   HORACE
>
>   Yeah, just like this brochure said, huh?

Horace fumbles through his pockets for the brochure,
can't find it. He joins up with Sam who wanders away
looking at map.

>   SAM
>
>   Others may have searched long before us,
>   but I think that we caught the right
>   bus.

Sam looks closely at the map.

>   Hmmm, looks like we're close. See this
>   cave, and that huge boulder? Now, if we
>   could just find this first marker right
>   here.

Sam points at map, we pull back to see huge cactus behind them shaped like an arrow pointing off in one direction.

EXT — DESERT — DAY

Sam and Horace plodding through desert, heads hung low in the glaring sun.

> HORACE
>
> Aw, we're going in circles, Sam, ain't we? Aren't we there yet, I'm hungry. What time is it? I have to go to the bathroom.

> SAM
>
> Knock it off, Junior, we've only been walking for ten minutes, for crying out loud!

> HORACE
>
> Where's the road, anyway? Why are we walking through sand and dirt and — OUCH! — cactus?

> SAM
>
> Because the map says Little 'Dorado is this way. Besides, I couldn't find it. We must've wandered too far in that sand storm last night.

> HORACE
>
> This is all your fault.

> SAM
>
> What is?

> HORACE
>
> This! Us starving to death out in the hot sun and sand while those canaries with thyroid problems fly overhead.

He points overhead to the circling vultures. Sam looks up, squinting into the sky.

> SAM
>
> Hmmm. That one on the left looks like he isn't going to wait too much longer on you.

Looks back down to Horace, finally hears what he said.

                    SAM

     My fault?

                 HORACE

     Yeah, "Let's go see Mexico" you said.

                    SAM

     And I suppose I'm the one who messed up
     the "Dr. Donavan Cures the Blind" rou-
     tine, huh, and got us chased across four
     counties?

                 HORACE

     It's not my fault I have fast reflexes
     and caught the change purse that lady
     dropped.

                    SAM

     You caught it before it fell out of her
     purse.

                 HORACE

     I was hungry.

                    SAM

     You were stupid.

                 HORACE

     I can do both at the same time, You were
     taking too long with the hook.

                    SAM

     We're not thieves, boy, they have
     to give it to us. We don't steal from
     anybody who don't deserve it.

                 HORACE

     Oh, Yeah?

                    SAM

     Yeah.

                 HORACE

     No, I mean "Oh, yeah," I forgot.

                    SAM

     You know what your problem is, Horace?

                              HORACE

          I'm hungry and stupid?

A donkey wagon pulls up behind them as Horace speaks.
MINERVA GONZALEZ — a young woman, ruggedly beautiful
— and her father, DUSTY — a kindly looking man in his
seventies, are in the wagon.

                              MINERVA

          You boys got some trouble?

Sam and Horace stop dead and gawk at Minerva. Dusty
chuckles and waves

                               SAM

          Hell-O.

                              HORACE

          Woof.

                              MINERVA

          I asked if you boys are in any kinda
          trouble. Need some help?

                               SAM

          Uh, how do, ma'am. My name is Sam, Sam
          Donavan. This is my partner Horace
          Fletcher, Say hello, Horace.

                              HORACE

          (gawks brainlessly) Gaaa.

                              DUSTY

          Your friend seems to be suffering from
          heat stroke or malaria.

                               SAM

          No, that's just the way he dresses
          himself.

                              MINERVA

          Are y'all lost or something? Nobody gets
          this far from town without a horse.

                               SAM

          Lost? Uh, well, yes we are, matter of
          fact. Town? What town is close by,
          Ma'am?

                    MINERVA

          You boys obviously ain't from around
          here. Little 'Dorado's the only civili-
          zation for fifty miles in any direction.

Nods toward back of wagon

          Hop in, we'll ride you back with us.

Sam and Horace exchange excited glances at the name
"Little 'Dorado". They climb into the wagon. Dusty
looks over his shoulder at them smiling

                    DUSTY

          I like your duds, you boys from back
          East?

                    HORACE

          Do we act like we're a couple of city
          slickers or something? (excited) Ooh,
          Sam! Look, prairie dogs!

Horace points out toward desert where three tortoises
eat cactus flowers. One looks up in their direction,
then turns to the other two.

                    TORTOISE 1

          That's them.

                    TORTOISE 2

          Shmucks.

The other tortoise looks at them, they resume eating,

                    MINERVA

          (to Dusty) We got a couple of live ones
          here, pop.

She shouts to the donkeys to "gidapp" and the wagon
rolls off.

EXT — LITTLE 'DORADO — DAY

Minerva's wagon pulls into town. It is a bustling town
of the late 1800's. People pass by on horses, cowboys
wander about, wagons etc.

Minerva and company pull up to the front of Dirty Glass
hotel/saloon and stop. Minerva turns to Sam and Horace.

                    MINERVA

          Alright, this as far as you go with me.

                    HORACE & SAM

She must be talking to you.

                         SAM

Ouch, I didn't even get to kiss her.

                       HORACE

Let the master handle this, Grandpa.
Look sister,

                      MINERVA

OUT.

                       HORACE

We're gittin' out here, so don't try to
keep us from gittin'.

                         SAM

Smooth.

Sam and Horace exit the wagon clumsily and watch as it
pulls away. They look around the street, then at each
other.

                         SAM

    Say, Junior, you notice anything funny
    about this town?

                       HORACE

    I haven't noticed anything funny at all
    right up to now.

They both look directly into the camera, then back out
around them.

                         SAM

    Not funny Ha Ha; funny strange

                       HORACE

    What's the difference?

                         SAM

    Horses, wagons, cowboy hats, no cars,
    no streetlights - nothing modern or
    progressive.

                       HORACE

    Well, this IS Texas.

                    SAM

        No, aside from that. This street isn't
        even paved, it's weird.

                    HORACE

        Compare it to your date with the Wheeler
        Twins in Denver.

                    SAM

        Weirder.

They think a beat, look at each other, shudder

                SAM AND HORACE

        Yeeeaah!

Sam looks over his shoulder at saloon sign and jerks
his thumb in its direction.

                    SAM

        Let's see what's doing in there. Maybe
        we can get some information.

                    HORACE

        Yeah, like where the gold is!

                    SAM

        Use some tact, Junior.

                    HORACE

        Why? I haven't got a bulletin board.

Sam and Horace swing through doors into saloon.

INT — SALOON — DAY

The saloon is fairly full. It is smokey, people are
drinking, gambling, piano music plays loudly out of
tune.

The piano player, STICKS — tall, lanky and handsome,
nicely dressed — checks out Sam and Horace, who head up
to the bar and talk to the bartender, SHOTGLASS — in
his fifties, stocky, take-no-shit air about him.

                  SHOTGLASS

        What'll ya have, boys?

                    SAM

        Oh, a little information's all, right

now, barkeep. How's a guy get a room
around these parts?

                    SHOTGLASS

Room's a dollar and a quarter a night —
pay in advance. No smokin', no shootin',
no pets.

Glares at Horace suspiciously on "No pets"

                    SAM

It's okay, he's housebroken. And, uh,
where could we find some, well, new
clothes?

                    SHOTGLASS

There's Mr. Hugo's 'cross the street.
Tell him I sent you an' he'll fix you up.
I don't know about him.

Nods at Horace.

                    HORACE

We're new in town.

                    SHOTGLASS

The hell you say? Really?

                    HORACE

That hot little number with the old man
dropped us off. We're lookin' for the
hidden gold, I guess you might call us a
couple o'prosecutors.

                    SHOTGLASS

That'd be "prospectors."

                    HORACE

I don't put things off, I'm just a
little... slow.

                    SAM

We ain't looking for no gold, mister,
we're just passing through, going to
Mexico on vacation.

Sam stomps on Horace's foot.

                    HORACE

Yeah, and first, OUCH!

                    SAM

    Like I said, we're just passing through.

                  SHOTGLASS

    Good, 'Cause if you was looking for
    gold, yer in the wrong place, San Fran-
    sisco'd be what you want. Er mebbe the
    Yukon. And if you know what's good fer
    ya both, y'all'd keep away from miss
    Minerva, she's Bart Tanner's girl.

                   HORACE

    "Bart Tanner"? What kinda stupid name is
    that? Sounds like a short, bald guy with
    a pug nose.

At the name Bart Tanner, the music stops, all eyes turn
to Horace and Sam. A few seconds later heavy footfalls
are heard outside the door.

The door swings open and BART TANNER — short, balding,
bully — walks in and stands close to Horace. All eyes
turn to Bart.
He scowls and looks around the saloon, his gaze stops
at Horace.

                   HORACE

    Heh heh, you'd be Bart Tanner, with my
    luck. (a beat) Nothing wrong with your
    nose, heh heh. Do I know you?

Bart glares a moment or two at Horace, just barely
notices him before he shouts at Sticks.

                    BART

    Ha'come t'aint no music and laughin'?
    Somebody say ta stop?

                   STICKS

    Not at all, Bart. Just takin' a little
    break's all.

                    BART

    Stop takin' a break. Play. You there;
    Laugh. You two; Play cards. You; Slap
    his face. The rest o'y'all keep on doin'
    what you're doin'.

At his cues, the addressed people do as instructed
until it looks as it did before Bart entered. He struts
up to bar next to Sam

> BART

Shotglass. Set me up. It's mah last day
as a bachelor; I'm a-fixin' ta aks Minerva t'marry me tomarra.

> SHOTGLASS

Ya don't say, Bart.

> BART

Mebbe you didn't hear me, ya dumb '49er,
I jes' DID say.

> SHOTGLASS

I heard ya, Bart. That's great.

He gets Bart a mug, fills it with Whiskey. Bart eyes Sam
and Horace and takes an instant dislike to them.

> BART

Who these city slickers, Shotglass? They
need some milk or sump'n?

> SHOTGLASS

They ain't nobody, Bart. Fact is, they's
just leaving.

> HORACE

No, we were just asking about the.

Sam clamps a hand over Horace's mouth and yanks him
away from the bar.

> SAM

Yep, that's right, leavin'.

> BART

Har! Dern slickers! Not a spine in the
lot o'em. Where's my whiskey?

Shotglass tops off the mug, slides it to Bart. Bart
gulps it down, wipes his mouth on his sleeve.

> BART

AAAAH!

Sam and Horace back off and head past the piano. Sticks
whispers to them as they pass.

STICKS

You boys really jus' passing through?

SAM

You talking to us?

STICKS

Well, I am talking to you. Does your
friend understand English?

Nods toward Horace, who tries to play it cool.

HORACE

I get by.

STICKS

No money? Need a place to pass the
night?

SAM

As fortune would have it, we are tempo-
rarily low on funds.

STICKS

Go out the back. You can sack out in the
shed next to the livery stable across
the alley. But ya'll'd better clear out
come sun up, Bart don't care much for
strangers.

SAM

Gee, thanks, brother, thank you.

STICKS

Don't mention it. I'll try to bring
something to eat later.

HORACE

Oh, I can't eat 'till Monday, he gets
weekends.

Sticks side-eyes him.

STICKS

You sure he's alright?

SAM

Don't mind Horace, he got kicked in the
head as a boy.

                         STICKS

     Oh, I'm sorry. Cow?

                         HORACE

     Mom.

                         STICKS

     Anyway, folks call me Sticks. Y'all best
     git now, 'fore Bart starts in.

                         SAM

     Thanks again. I'm Sam, this is Horace.
     We'll see you later.

Sam and Horace duck out the back. Sticks looks
nervously toward Bart, who is downing another mug of
whiskey and abusing various people at the bar.

EXT — STREET — DAY

Sam and Horace amble out into the street from the
alley.

                         SAM

     We're still here, Horace. It wasn't just
     a dream, we really must have gone back
     in time or something.

                         HORACE

     Oh lay off with the time thing already,
     willya, Sam. Even I'M not dumb enough to
     fall for that. You said yourself that
     this was a tourist trap. This is all
     just for show, it's play-acting.

Sam looks down at Horace's feet.

                         SAM

     Watch where you're walking, boy, you
     just stepped in some play-acting.

Horace looks down, makes a face, lifts up his foot.

                         HORACE

     Aw, sh...oot.

Looks back up.

     That must have been some dog.

Horace starts to wipe his foot on the ground when he
sees Minerva down the street.

                    HORACE

          Hey, there's that cute little taxi driv-
          er that's crazy about me. Let's go ask
          her about the hidden treasure.

They walk over toward Minerva, who is coming from a
general store carrying a large sack of corn flour.

                    SAM

          Good day, ma'am. Can we help you with
          that?

                    MINERVA

          Howdy boys, stickin' around awhile? (to
          Sam) No thanks, I don't know about back
          East, but we Texas women can handle our-
          selves.

                    HORACE

          Nonsense, sister, just our way of saying
          thank'ee for the ride yesterday.

                    MINERVA

          Well, thank you kindly, here.

She drops sack into Horace's arms. He drops to the
ground like a hunk of lead.

                    HORACE

          What do you have in here, big huge
          blocks of lead?

                    MINERVA

          Just corn meal, I don't get into town
          but once a month, so I gotta buy bulk.

                    HORACE

          Well, give me the bag of bulk, you can
          take this cornmeal. I prefer to carry it
          when it's shaped like muffins.

While the following conversation takes place, Horace is
struggling with the sack of cornmeal, trying to get it
into the wagon.

                    SAM

          Yes ma'am, we decided to stick around a
          while. Thought we'd see about that leg-
          end.

MINERVA

And, what, legend would that be?

SAM

That old legend about the lost treasure
from the city of gold. They say there's
a fortune hidden somewhere hereabouts.

MINERVA

That old story? Why, that's just a silly fib cooked up to keep folks comin' to
Little 'Dorado for the trade. Used to be
real gold here, a little, in the hills,
but no more. Truth is, this town's on
it's way out. If you both had any real
sense, you'd be doing likewise.

SAM

Just a silly story, huh? Well, then I
guess you can't blame us for trying.

They watch Horace for a few seconds.

Say, there any games of chance in this
town?

MINERVA

Gamblin'? Sure, over to the "Dirty
Glass," that's the saloon we dropped you
off at last night. If Bart ain't play-
in' , you'll get a fair game, if you kin
handle that.

SAM

I think we can deal with that. Thanks
again, ma'am.

Minerva smiles and offers her hand to Sam.

MINERVA

Minerva. Minerva Gonzales. I ain't old
enough t'be called "Ma'am". You're Sam?

Sam shakes her hand softly.

SAM

That I am, Sam Donavan.

MINERVA

Well, Sam Donavan, after you win big,

> get yourself some new duds. (Looks them
> over) You two stick out like coyotes in
> a hen house in those.

>> SAM

> Yes, I guess these do rather not fit the
> scenery.

He looks down at his clothes, then up to where Minerva
was, she is now over by Horace.

> So, after I change, how about you and me
> go get a

Minerva picks up sack from Horace with no problem, puts
in into wagon.

>> MINERVA

> Maybe some other time, Sam.

To Horace on ground.

> Thanks. I'll be seeing you, I guess.

She gets into the wagon and heads off down the street.
Horace stands up, dusting himself off.

>> HORACE

> What, only one bag?

>> SAM

> Come on, Junior, let's go make some
> money.

>> HORACE

> You found a press?

>> SAM

> HONEST money.

>> HORACE

> "Honest money"?

He stops, pulls a card from his coat and reads it. On
it is printed "Honest money = hard work." Horace puts
it back in his pocket and sighs despondently.

> Oh, fffuuuudge

He follows Sam into saloon.

INT — SALOON — DAY

Sam and Horace approach a card table where two MEN and
two WOMEN sit playing poker.

                         SAM

          Room for one more?

                      WOMAN 1

          Sure, stranger. Buy-in's fifty dollars.

                         SAM

          Well, I was hoping.

Looking Sam up and down, smiles wolfishly.

                      WOMAN 1

          So was I. But I think we'll let that go
          for a hand or two, you look like a win-
          ner to me.

                         SAM

          Thank you kindly, ma'am, I appreciate
          it, I'll get you after I win.

                      WOMAN 1

          Unless I get you first.

                      HORACE

          Hey, can I play?

                         ALL

          NO.

Sam gets a hurt look from Horace.

                         SAM

          I'm sorry, boy, but these are big stakes
          here, this isn't Old Maid or Go Fish
          we're playing.

                      HORACE

          Oh, good, then it ought to be easy.

                         SAM

          Besides, you don't have the buy-in.

                       MAN 1

          Aw, let the guy play, he ain't gonna win
          nuthin'.

                        WOMAN 1

          Alright, sit down, son.

                        HORACE

          Ooh, can I get some of those!

Points at colored poker chips.

                        WOMAN 2

          Sure, honey, here's a few you can play
          with.

She drops fifty dollars worth in front of him.

                        WOMAN 1

          Game's Five Card Draw, ace's wild, mini-
          mum five dollar bet.

Everyone antes up, woman 1 deals. Everyone looks at
their cards and shuffles them around. To Horace.

          Starts with you, handsome

She winks at him.

                        HORACE

          You said aces are wild?

                        WOMAN 1

          That's right, sugar.

Horace slaps his cards down face up on the table.

                        HORACE

          GIN.

                        MAN 2

          Gonna be a long game.

                        SAM

          It usually is.

EXT — STREET — DAY

In front of barber shop, Minerva is sitting in the
wagon, waiting for Dusty. Bart comes up behind her.

                        BART

          Mornin' sweetie!

                        MINERVA

          Good morning, Bart, what do you want?

                    BART

Why, that ain't no way ta talk to yer
fiancee.

                  MINERVA

You ain't my fiancee, Bart.

                    BART

Well, now, one word from you would
change all that, now wouldn't it?

                  MINERVA

I'm thinkin' of one word, it's got two
letters.

Bart stops a minute to think of the possibilities, but
gets frustrated.

                    BART

Come off it, Minerva, what's amatter with
me for a husband? I think yer as pretty
as a wagon full o' fresh kilt rabbits.

                  MINERVA

How elegant. I don't suppose your thinking my daddy has gold hidden somewhere
around here has anything to do with your
attraction to me, does it?

                    BART

Gold?! Naw, does he? 'cause it don' matter even if he did, but,

Dusty exits the barber shop and sees them.

                   DUSTY

No, I don't.

                  MINERVA

Pop, you ready to go?

                   DUSTY

Yeah, I'm done, and you can drag your
worthless hide out of here too, Tanner.
Or are you gonna follow us allover cre-
ation until you drop in the desert like
your Daddy did?

                         BART

          You crazy old man. My pappy shoulda put
          a hole in you thirty years ago, and may-
          be I oughtta.

                        MINERVA

          Oh, too bad, Bart; I was just about to
          say yes to your lovely offer.

Bart boils up to his ears. He turns and stomps away,
seething. Minerva watches until Bart turns a corner out
of sight.

                        MINERVA

          Let's go, Pop, I got some flowers.

She pulls flowers out of back of wagon, shows them to
Dusty.

          She'll like these.

                         DUSTY

          Who likes those?

                        MINERVA

          Ma, were going to put these on her
          grave, remember?

Looks at him closely.

          Oh, you gone again, Pop?

Puts arm around him gently.

                        MINERVA

          I'll tell her you was thinking about her
          today, okay?

                         DUSTY

          We going for a ride again?

She helps Dusty board the wagon and they drive off.

A few moments later Bart and two FLUNKIES on horseback
appear from behind a building, they exchange glances
and ride after Dusty and Minerva.

INT — SALOON CARD TABLE — DAY

Sam and Horace play cards. Everyone except Horace has
only a few chips left. Horace has a great pile of them,
there is also a huge pile in the "pot" which Horace has
just won.

Woman 2 leans toward Sam, muttering out of the side of her mouth.

> WOMAN 2

> He been cheatin' or something? I never seen anyone that thick in the head win so much.

> SAM

> (dumbfounded) That's the sad part, I was cheating, he doesn't know how.

> MAN 1

> You were cheatin'? I was cheating too.

> WOMAN 1 AND MAN 2

> Me too.

They all turn stunned at Horace as he rakes in the pot.

> HORACE

> Woo! What a fun game. Less stress than solitaire, and you get paid too!

To woman 2.

> Oh. Here's 'that buy-in you floated me. And I guess I'll have to cover Sam too, seeing as he's a big loser today. Yessiree Bob, I may even get the woman this time, too.

Leers at woman 2, winks; she slaps him.

> Or not. Just a thought.

Horace gloats, the others rub their heads and slap the table.

EXT — TOWN STREET — DAY

Sam and Horace walk down sidewalk. Horace is counting money. He hands Sam five dollars.

> HORACE

> Here's your share, Sam. Don't spend it all in one place, huh?

Sam looks at his bill, then at the wad in Horace's hands.

> SAM

> Wait a minute.

                    HORACE

        No, no, I want you to have it, Sam. I
        know you'd do the same for me.

                    SAM

        You're probably right there, boy, but
        who's gonna keep all the rest of that?
        Who's gonna invest it? Who's gonna

                    HORACE

        Not get another dime? YOU, That's who.
        It's about time old Horace Fletcher had
        his own bankroll.

                    SAM

        Don't be foolish, boy, you'll spend it
        all on nothing. You'll be broke in two
        days.

                    HORACE

        Not a chance, Sam. I've finally seen the
        light. You been pulling that old line on
        me for years, keeping me from saving any
        money at all. Well this time I'll have
        money to spare long after I buy a ticket
        to "No Sam Land".

Horace spots a man with a pony across the street and
stops dead.

        Oh boy, a pony! Think he'll give us a
        ride? A ride, what am I saying. I can
        buy the whole pony.

Horace looks over at Sam, then down at the money. He
hands it all over to Sam.

                    SAM

        You're doing the right thing, Boy. Now
        let's go get some duds.

INT — MR. HUGO'S — DAY

Sam and Horace enter and are met by an attendant,
WINFIELD — a snobby gentleman — who looks them both up
and down.

                    WINFIELD

        May I help you?

                    SAM

> Yes, my good man, you may. My associ-
> ate and I lost our luggage on the stage-
> coach, and find ourselves in need of some
> attire more in keeping with this partic-
> ular region's fashion and functionality.

The attendant looks at them, Horace bends forward.

                    HORACE

> I just want to look like I came
> from here.

                    WINFIELD

> Impossible.

                    SAM

> Well, just do your best, then. I'm a 38
> regular.

Sam puts his arms out to his sides. Winfield starts to measure.

MONTAGE

- Sam and Horace trying on different sets of clothes

- Sam always gets sharp looking outfits

- Horace looks like a dope in everything he picks out

- Even in the same outfit

END MONTAGE

Sam and Horace stand dressed in satisfactory suits of the era. Sam wears "city clothes," Horace wears an idiot's version of "cowboy duds." Sam stands looking himself in a full length mirror.

                    SAM

> Not bad, not bad at all, Winfield. Thank
> you very much. Just have the rest of
> my things wrapped and sent over to the
> Dirty Glass, would you?

He hands a ten dollar bill to Winfield, who accepts it greedily and pockets it.

                    WINFIELD

> Yes SIR! And thank you sir!

Horace gives the attendant a one dollar piece.

                    HORACE
        Likewise.

                    WINFIELD
        You only purchased the one
        outfit, "sir."

                    HORACE
        Well, then send over three more just
        like it.

Winfield sneers and goes to wrap the parcels. Sam and

Horace head out into the street.

EXT — STREET — DAY

Sam and Horace cross the street back to the saloon

                    SAM
        Well, Junior, let's go get a room, then
        plan out our next endeavor. You know, I
        could get used to this.

                    HORACE
        Me too. I could get real used to this!

We hear a squish, Horace and Sam look down at Horace's
feet and make a face.

                    HORACE
        'Course, some things take more getting
        used to than others.

They walk on, Horace hopping and trying to clean his
shoe.

INT — DIRTY GLASS SALOON — DAY

Sam and Horace are at bar with Shotglass, Sam gives
Shotglass some money.

                    SAM
        Okay, barkeep, here's for a room for
        each of us for two nights, and a little
        something for the broken bathroom door.

                    SHOTGLASS
        What broken bathroom door?

                    SAM

     (glances at Horace) It's early yet...
     trust me.

Shotglass turns to a young woman, ANNA, in a housemaid
dress.

                 SHOTGLASS

     Anna, show this gentleman and his friend
     to their rooms. Then run over to the
     carpenter and have him get a new bath-
     room door ready.

                    ANNA

     Walk this way, please.

Horace and Sam watch her walk away from them, Sam
whistles softly, Horace gawks.

                   HORACE

     If I could walk that way, I'd have a lot
     more friends.

                    SAM

     In prison, maybe.

They follow her up the stairs and start down the hall.
Anna stops and points as she hands them keys.

                    ANNA

     Your rooms are 14 and 13.

Horace gets key 13.

     There's clean towels and wash basins in
     the rooms, bathroom is at the end of the
     hall. If you need anything else, I'm
     downstairs. Dinner's at six.

                    SAM

     Thank you, miss.

                   HORACE

     Yeah, thanks, and here.

He hands her some PAPER money.

     get yourself something nice.

She looks at the money wide-eyed.

                    ANNA
        Oh, sir... I... this is too much.
                    HORACE
        Is it?

He snatches it back, hands her a COIN.

                    HORACE
        Here then, get yourself something cheap.

Anna glares and leaves. Sticks passes them on his way
downstairs.

                    STICKS
        Hiya boys, what's doin'?

                    SAM
        Sticks, just the guy we need to talk
        to. We just got a room, figured we hang
        around awhile.

                    HORACE
        Yeah, and we thought we'd...

                    STICKS
        I'll tell you boys something, 'cause I
        like y'all. If you're stickin' around to
        look for that treasure you heard about

To Horace

        I heard you babblin' 'bout it yesterday
        at the bar, you'll be wastin' your time,
        and making no friend of Bart.

                    HORACE
        Well, then, maybe we could...

                    STICKS
        And y'all don't want to try anything
        with Miz Minerva, 'cause you'll waste
        your time, and you'll make no friend of
        Bart. And Don't eat the Monday special
        from the kitchen.

                    HORACE
        Or we'll waste our time and make no
        friend of Bart?

                    STICKS

     No, it's just usually awful.

                     SAM

     Well. Thanks Sticks. Guess we'll just
     enjoy a little vacation.

                    STICKS

     Don't mention it.

To Horace

          What's with you, boy, looks like you
          forgot ta use the bathroom or something.

Horace's eyes widen as he remembers.

                   HORACE

     Bathroom!

He runs down the hall.

                     SAM

          Don't forget to open the...

We hear a loud CRASH and splintering of wood.

                     SAM

     ...door.

INT — MINERVA'S HOUSE — NIGHT

Minerva and Dusty sit at the table eating. Minerva (is
excited, Dusty pokes at his food.

                   MINERVA

          We found it today, Pop, we finally found
          it. Can you believe it?

                   DUSTY

     Found what?

                   MINERVA

          The GOLD, Papa, the treasure you hid
          almost thirty years ago.

                   DUSTY

     I did that? Where'd I git treasure?

                   MINERVA

          You used to tell me when I was little
          that you got in South America.

Thinks a few beats, looks at Dusty sadly.

> Oh Papa, we'll load it all in a wag-
> on and head on out of this little town.
> We'll have enough for you to live out
> your years comfortably, not breaking
> your back here just to get by. Worrying
> every day that someone'll find it. It'll
> be like it was when you were younger.

                    DUSTY

> Oh, yeah. When I was young. We had so
> much, your mother and I, what ever
> happened?

                    MINERVA

> Tanners. Old man Tanner and his boys.

There is a loud pounding on door. Bart, drunk, shouts
from other side.

                    BART

> Open up, lil' filly, this is yourn
> financee come a callin'.

Minerva pulls a gun from a cabinet, thinks, then hides
it under her napkin.

                    MINERVA

> Sit, Pop, let's find out how much he
> knows.

She rises slowly, heads toward door and opens it. Bart,
ready to pound again, stumbles in.

                    BART

> Well, now, lookee here, I'm jes' in time
> for dinner with the in-laws.

                    MINERVA

> What do you want, Bart?

                    BART

> I come t'aks you ta marry me one las'
> time, Minerva — then wit yer pappy's
> gold, we'll run this town, an' buy a few
> more! Ha!

                    DUSTY

> My GOLD? I ain't got no

                    BART

     Shaddap, ya crazy ol' bandicoot! Fer
     years you stuffed our ears with your
     stories. Now yer jes' fakin' losin' yer
     dad-blamed mind jes' so you don't

                  MINERVA

     That's enough, Tanner. You leave that
     poor man alone and get out right now. He
     ain't been the same since Ma died.

Bart reels drunkenly, smacks Minerva accidentally.
Minerva makes a fist and hauls back her arm.

                    BART

     Shut yer yap! I'll have his gold, and
     his daughter, or my name isn't Bart
     Tan...

A gunshot cuts him short. Bart and Minerva stop and
turn to see Dusty leveling Minerva's colt at Bart's
head.

                   DUSTY

     (steadily) I may be losin' my mind slow-
     ly, Tanner, but you'll be losin' yours a
     lot quicker the next time you touch my
     daughter. Now git.

Bart points at Dusty in an accusing manner.

                    BART

     I seen y'all out ta Rattler Crick today.

Points to Minerva.

     You marry me an' we'll share it. DON'T,
     an when I find it I'll burn this town to
     the ground and build a new city on yer
     graves.

He stumbles out. Minerva and Dusty relax and she takes
the pistol from Dusty. They sit.

                  MINERVA

     We have to act soon. He's close.

                   DUSTY

     Who is?

                    MINERVA

     Bart. He's gonna find it.

                    DUSTY

     Bart was here? What'd he want?

Minerva shakes her head and rises, she hugs Dusty from
behind.

EXT — SALOON — NIGHT

Sam and Horace leave the saloon after dinner, picking
their teeth. They walk past the shed where they spent
the previous evening.

                    SAM

          Imagine that, a nice girl like her mar-
          rying a boor like Bart Tanner. What's he
          got?

                    HORACE

          Looked like a Colt .45 and a bad atti-
          tude.

                    SAM

          I tell you, Junior, something weird is
          going on here. Look, I found it behind a
          crate in that old shed last night.

He indicates the shed, pulls a newspaper out of his
back pocket.

          Look at the date.

                    HORACE

          1881 - So - I've got old newspapers in
          my underwear drawer back in Piney Falls.

Sam looks at Horace for a moment, then gets back on
track.

                    SAM

          It's not even yellow.

                    HORACE

          My underwear?

                    SAM

          The Paper, this is like new, only a
          month or so old. Some of these stories
          are real events. It all fits!

                    HORACE

My underwear?

                     SAM

No! Forget about your underwear for
a minute. This town, the horses, the
clothes, this paper — I'm telling you,
Horace, we've gone back in time.

                    HORACE

Wow! How'd we do that?

                     SAM

Don't know, maybe that storm the other
night or something, but just imagine,
Junior, the Old West.

                    HORACE

Yeah! What?

                     SAM

It's just ripe for the picking. Why,
half our operations haven't even been
thought up yet, no cops, lots of gull-
ible folks, no police bulletins.

                    HORACE

No film?

They both turn slowly and look directly toward us.

                    HORACE

Oh good, they're still here.

They turn back away from us.

                     SAM

Junior, we can make a load of money
here. Maybe that lost gold isn't real,
but we'll make our fortunes anyway,
we'll live like kings!

                    HORACE

I ain't wearing' any tights.

                     SAM

You know, boy, there's a pile of boxes
and bottles in that shed. You still have
your bag?

> HORACE

Yeah, it's back in my room, why?

> SAM

What have we got left?

> HORACE

Some bandages, deck of cards, tools, and
a few tubes of that green stuff I found
last year on the beach in New York.

> SAM

I've got an idea. Go get the bag and
meet me back down in the shed. Here's
what we'll do

His voice trails off as they walk.

EXT — STREET — DAY

Sam and Horace are setting up a sidewalk table with a
box full of bottles filled with green liquid. A sign on
the box reads "Dr. Fletcher's Fabulous Snake-O!"

Some people pass by, others stop to look and listen.

> SAM

Theater's filling up, boy, let's put on a
show.

> HORACE

I just hope this stuff isn't lethal.

> SAM

Well, didn't you make it the way I told
you?

> HORACE

Yes, that's what's worrying me.

Sam winces, then turns back toward his audience.

> SAM

Step right up folks, in just a few moments, Dr. H. T. Fletcher will begin his
amazing story of Snake-O, that wondrous
cure from the Black Hills of the North
Dakota Territory, and how he, himself,
wrestled the secret from a powerful In-
dian Shaman.

HORACE

He was actually only a Junior Shaman, he
wasn't fully accredited yet.

SAM

At the end of Dr. Fletcher's disserta-
tion you will have the once-in-a-life-
time opportunity to purchase — for the
low, low introductory price of four bits
— an actual vial of the miraculous
potion itself!

HORACE

Don't say "vile", they might get the
right idea.

SAM

And "why" do you ask are we bringing
you this at such low cost? Why are we
offering this incredible inoculation at
inconceivable prices?

HORACE

Yeah, why are we?

SAM

It's simple

He picks up a bottle, opens it, sniffs it.

SAM

This is Snake-O, the wonder of oils, It
heals snake bites, cools fevers, and
simmers boils. You can't do without it,
it'll soothe your itchy rash. So just
take yourself a bottle, and we'll take
away your cash.

People try to get a better look, they "ooh" and "ahh"

HORACE

Easy now, please don't crowd the stage.

EXT — STREET — SAME TIME

Minerva and Dusty are on a sidewalk across the street.
They see Sam and Horace as people get in closer and
start asking questions.

                    DUSTY
          What's going on over there?

                   MINERVA
          Trouble.

Minerva thinks, does a slow double-take.

          Or maybe a solution.

                    DUSTY
          I want a glass of lemonade.

                   MINERVA
          O.K. Pop, come on, we'll get you a glass
          of lemonade.

Minerva leads Dusty away.

Sam and Horace get some takers, they talk with a WOMAN.

                    WOMAN
          Does that stuff really cure anything?

                    SAM
          Absolutely, why, I myself once had the
          worst stomach malady imaginable, and
          just thinking about drinking this con-
          coction made me feel ten times better!

                    MAN
          Will it do anything for baldness?

                   HORACE
          Sure! Massage it into your scalp and
          just see what happens with your hair.

                    SAM
          (under breath) No lies.

                   HORACE
          That's no lie. This stuff is the best
          ting for baldness. That guy who used it
          in Virginia went bald in two days.

Sam holds up a bottle, gesturing to the crowd.

                    SAM
          Ahem, Yes, ladies and gentlemen, Dr.
          Fletcher's Amazing Snake-O — ONLY four
          bits, fifty cents, one half of one

dollar — for a complete month's supply
in a handsome reusable container.

                    WOMAN

I'll take a bottle!

                    BALD MAN

I'll take two!

                    SAM

Pass the hat, Boy, the congregation
feels charitable.

                    HORACE

Yeah, let's just clear out in a day or
two, or they'll be passing this hat with
our heads still in it.

Horace holds out his hat as people throw money into it
and take bottles from Sam.

INT — SALOON — DAY

Minerva and Dusty enter the saloon and mosey on up to
the bar. Shotglass nods.

                    MINERVA

Set Dusty up, Shotglass.

                    SHOTGLASS

Sure, Minerva.

He shoots a glance to a table where Bart and his
buddies sit drinking and playing cards, then back to
Minerva.

Bart notices Minerva and Dusty, gets up and struts over
to them, talking loudly to the room.

                    BART

Well, lookee what we got here, if'n it
ain't Miss Minerva and her trained monkey. Hah yew, Minerva?

                    MINERVA

I'm just fine, Bart. You?

Looks at him and thugs over at table.

Ain't there no other old men and women
in town ta bother?

                         BART

          Oh, they is, we just wanta make sure we
          got it down on y'all fust! Hey, old man.

Pushes Dusty, goading him.

          You'n me got some unfinished biness. No
          side iron today.

                        DUSTY

          Why sure! I'll go t'the dance with you,
          Louise, just let me git my suit pressed.

Minerva laughs, Shotglass snickers. The thugs try to
keep from laughing.

Bart makes a fist and tries to hit Dusty, Minerva grabs
Bart's arm and holds it with little difficulty.

Shotglass pulls gun from beneath counter and levels it
at Bart.

                      SHOTGLASS

          Not in here, Tanner.

Bart wrenches his arm free, shrugs, then throws an
air-punch at Shotglass and snarls.

                         BART

          You next, beer-slinger!

                      SHOTGLASS

          You call it, Tanner, but like I said,
          not in here. Clear on out. (to thugs)
          You too.

There is a stand-off for a few seconds, then Bart backs
down.

                         BART

          Let's ride, boys. I think I'd like ta
          see what's doin' down ta Rattler Crick.

Glares at Minerva, then whirls around and exits; gang
follows, sniggering.

                       MINERVA

          I'm sorry, Shotglass.

                      SHOTGLASS

          I can handle myself, Minerva, you just
          worry about yourself and Mr. Dusty. I'm

thinking Bart's gittin' a bit tetched in
the head.

                    MINERVA

     Me too. Drink up Pop.

Dusty drinks his lemonade, Minerva stares out toward
the thugs.

EXT — STREET — DAY

Sam and Horace walk toward the saloon. They see Bart
and his boys storming loudly down the street. Horace
holds the satchel in one hand, weighing it.

                    HORACE

          Hoo-boy, Sam, you were right. I must
          have at least twenty dollars here. Is
          that good?

Sam talks as they walk up and into the saloon.

INT — SALOON — DAY

                    SAM

          It's the 1800's, Horace, that's like two
          hundred back where we're from! I've got
          thirty dollars in advanced sales, we'll
          have to mix some more tonight, then
          we'll buy a stage ticket to a bigger
          city and ...

They spy Minerva and Dusty at bar.

                    SAM

          Oh-ho, look here, boy. Good afternoon,
          Minerva, sir.

                    DUSTY

     Howdy fellas.

                    MINERVA

          Oh, good day, gentlemen. I see you
          didn't waste any time finding gainful
          employment.

                    SAM

     Well, you gotta live, right, Junior?

                    HORACE

     That's right, so you might as well do

> it in comfort. We'll pick up their tab,
> barkeep, and a free round for the house
> on us!

He spins around with a flourish, the saloon is empty except for them.

> Make it the good stuff!

> SHOTGLASS

> There ain't no "house" to serve.

> HORACE

> Ahh, their loss, my gain. Hit me with a
> Ginger Ale, neat.

> MINERVA

> Sasparilla, Shotglass.

Shotglass pulls out a brown bottle and blows three years worth of dust off it. He opens it and pours into a glass.

> MINERVA

> Say, Sam,

> SAM

> Yes?

> MINERVA

> Sam, I was thinking, uh, Pop, why don't
> you take your lemonade to go

> DUSTY

> Go where? MINERVA Just outside, Pop.

She nods in Sam's direction. I need to discuss some business with Sam and his partner, Okay?

Dusty looks to Sam, then past him to Horace who is gagging on his sasparilla.

> DUSTY

> Sure honey, I'll be right outside then.

> MINERVA

> Thanks, pop. Dusty waddles out of saloon
> with his lemonade.

EXT — SALOON SIDEWALK — CONTINUOUS

Dusty exits the saloon, and walks down the street. Bart

skulks around the corner in the alley. He nods to a
flunky across the street, who heads after Dusty.

Bart grins a nasty grin as he nods to himself and
lights a cigar.

INT — SALOON — CONTINUOUS

Sam, Horace, Minerva and Shotglass are at the bar.

> MINERVA
>
> Listen Sam, Horace, I need to talk to
> you, we need your help.

> SAM
>
> We?

> MINERVA
>
> Dusty and me.

> HORACE
>
> Let's talk.

Minerva looks to Shotglass who is cleaning the counter
or glasses or some such bartendery thing, then glances
to a table near a window.

> MINERVA
>
> Over here, it's more private.

> HORACE
>
> I thought Brandysnifter was a friend of
> yours?

> MINERVA
>
> Oh, Shotglass is okay, but what I have
> to tell you, well, the fewer people who
> know about it, the better.

> HORACE
>
> This is it, she wants me.

> SAM
>
> You? You're short and stupid.

> HORACE
>
> You don't have to convince me, tell her
> my qualities.

> MINERVA
>
> I'm telling you guys because it's obvi-

ous you already know how to play on the
sly. If I cut you a piece you'll more'n
likely be happily on your way; especially when folks start usin' that stuff you
been selling.

She eyes the satchel, Horace pulls it close and sinks
in his chair.

                    SAM

        She's on to us boy. Look, Minerva; we
        don't hurt anyone; we're just trying to
        get by like everyone else. Oh, sure, it
        may be some time before the effects wear
        off - but the stuff we do is mostly harm-
        less.

                    HORACE

        Sure, sure, why that guy in Ohio's due
        out of the coma any day now.

                    SAM

        You're not helping.

                    MINERVA

        I understand all that. That's why I
        think we can trust you. You help us move
        it, and we'll give you enough to keep
        you going for a while.

                    HORACE

        Move it? Give us what?

                    SAM

        The Gold. It is the gold isn't it? Min-
        erva, there really is gold hidden in
        this town, you and Dusty found it.

                    MINERVA

        Shhh. Yes.

                    HORACE

        (jumps up, excited) Whoa!

Shotglass eyes him.

        Heh, heh, that's how I get my horse to
        stop. "Whoa" I says to him, heh heh.

Horace sits back down.

MINERVA

It belongs to my family. When I was a little girl my father and mother would take me out to a secret cave where their treasure was hidden. I used to play with all that shiny stuff.

HORACE

You need any playmates?

MINERVA

They'd tell me stories of El Dorado, the city of gold, somewhere in South America.

SAM

Yeah, I've heard of that. It doesn't really exist.

MINERVA

It does. Years before I was born, my father stumbled into the city after a hunting party he was with was all but killed off by illness. The people of the city nursed him back to health.

HORACE

Sounds like they saved his bankroll from extinction, too.

SAM

Let her finish, Horace, this is a long monologue.

MINERVA

Later, he saved the life of the king's daughter. To thank my father, the king gave him enough gold for three lifetimes, and the hand of his daughter in marriage.

HORACE

Wow, Aunt Margie was right. Bravery does get rewarded. And me a coward.

Sam waves quickly at Horace.

                    SAM

Hush. (To Minerva) Go on, what happened
then?

                  MINERVA

My parents left the city a year later
and settled on my father's ranch here
in Texas. The ranch prospered and grew
until this town, Little 'Dorado, was
born. But soon after that my mother
became very ill and died.

                    SAM

Oh, I'm sorry to hear that.

                  HORACE

Who got her gold?

                    SAM

That's enough, Horace.

                  MINERVA

Thank you, Sam. It was a long time ago.

                    SAM

Wow, so you're sort of like a princess?

                  HORACE

Wow, so you're sort of like loaded?

She stares into Sam's eyes a moment, then she pulls her
gaze away.

                  MINERVA

Here's where I need your help. Bart and
his boys have been after our treasure
for years — Bart's father used to follow
Dusty every time he went out for a ride,
just hopin' to come upon the treasure so
he could steal it. My father spent so
many years trying to outwit old man Tanner, that he eventually outwitted himself. But now Bart's getting close, and
he's a lot meaner than his old man ever
was. We need to move it to a big city
and put it in a bank.

                    HORACE

Sounds like your life won't be too uncomfortable either.

                    MINERVA

I'm prepared to give you both enough
to live on so you won't have to hustle
small towns anymore.

                    HORACE

Well then, I'm prepared to accept that.
I'll take tens and twenties.

                    SAM

Wipe that drool off your chin, Horace.
Now, let me get this strait, we help you
move the gold to ...

                    MINERVA

I don't know, maybe San Antonio...

                    SAM

...to San Antonio, you put it in a bank,
and we get to leave you with our pockets
full?

                    MINERVA

That's right, and here's what we'll do

She trails off.

EXT — SALOON, WINDOW NEAR MINERVA — SAME TIME

Bart, just outside the window, smiles and nods as he
listens, then he spits out the stub of his cigar and
hurries away.

INT — SALOON, MINERVA'S TABLE — SAME TIME

                    MINERVA

And then, with your pockets full, you
can leave.

                    HORACE

Remind me to see the tailor to have more
pockets installed.

                    SAM

I don't know that I like that
arrangement.

                    HORACE

     Exactly, why if I, WHAT? Sam, didn't you
     hear what she said? Gold. Full pockets,
     all the women we can carry.

                    MINERVA

     What?

                    HORACE

     I just threw that last one in myself.

                    SAM

     Oh, I heard. I just don't know if I like
     the leaving part. I'm kinda attached to
     Minerva's face, it's started to grow on
     me.

                    HORACE

     Why you two-faced, what about me? You're
     just gonna dump me? After all these
     years, what's a matter with my face,
     anyway?

Both Sam and Minerva look slowly to Horace, look back
to each other, shudder, take each others hands.

                    HORACE

     Oh I'm not that weird-looking, why in
     grade school I was voted Most Likely to
     Break into a Gallop.

                    MINERVA

     Shucks, Sam, do you really mean it? It's
     not, not just because of ...

                    SAM

     The money? No, no, no, I've had plenty
     of money in my time.

                    HORACE

     Yeah, and who made it for you?

                    SAM

     And I've known plenty of women, too.

                    HORACE

     Dr. Frankenstein made those.

                         SAM

     Can, can I get you a drink, would you
     like to go somewhere and talk?

                       MINERVA

     Sure, Sam.

                       HORACE

     Hey, where are you two going? Oh, not
     that, that's not fair.

They get up and walk to the bar. Horace sits dejected
at table sipping sasparilla and gagging.

Sticks enters from staircase and sits by Horace.

                       STICKS

     Whatsamatter, boy, you look like you
     just lost a bet.

                       HORACE

     No, I'm just trying to figure out how to
     kill a rat.

                       STICKS

     Huh?

                       HORACE

     Nothing.

                       STICKS

     Hey, (indicating Sam) he's doing pretty
     good.

                       HORACE

     No he isn't.

                       STICKS

     Sure he is.

                       HORACE

     I do "pretty good", but she likes him.
     That means he's the best.

                       STICKS

      Or you really stink.

Horace glares at him.

                         HORACE
          Yeah.

Minerva and Sam, with drinks, turn to leave the saloon.
                         STICKS
          Hey, Sam, y'all really oughtn't be
          spending time with miz Minerva,
          Bart'll...

                         MINERVA
          Bart'll nothing, Sticks. Dusty and I are
          leaving town soon, were going to...

Sticks shakes his head and waves his hands and sits
back down next to Horace.

                         STICKS
          Don't tell me. I got no threshold for
          pain and Bart'd just whoop it outta me.

Thinks a beat.
          As a matter o' fact, guess I'll be mov-
          in' on too, head back to Oh, you still
          here, Horace?

                         HORACE
          I don't know, ask the headliner.

Nods angrily at Sam.

                         SAM
          Oh, come off it Junior, you knew someday
          we'd have to go our separate ways. We
          knew I'd meet the right woman some day,
          and you'd, you'd, have to go away, or
          something.

                         MINERVA
          Let me talk to him Sam. You tell Sticks
          the plan, he's Okay.

                         HORACE
          Yeah, then you'll all have a good laugh
          on me. Thanks for nothin', Sam.

                         MINERVA
          Come with" me, Horace.

Sam and Sticks start to talk at the table. Minerva and Horace exit.

EXT — SALOON SIDEWALK — DAY

Horace and Minerva walk down the sidewalk.

> HORACE
>
> What are you going to do now, send me to my room?

> MINERVA
>
> Come on, now, Horace, I just want to talk to you. You seem upset.

> HORACE
>
> Upset? I'm about a mile and a half past upset.

> MINERVA
>
> Let's walk a bit.

She takes his arm as they walk out of frame. One of Bart's cronies appears in the alley and looks after them, then returns to the shadows.

> MINERVA
>
> I know how you must feel, Horace, losing Sam and all, but you have to understand that sometimes men and women fall in love and they, go away together and

> HORACE
>
> (Mocking) "Sometimes men and women fall in love and go away," What am I, some kind of kid, you have to talk to me like that? I've been out of short britches for going on five years now and I, ooh! Candy!

He spots candy in store window and stops to stare with nose and hands pressed on the glass.

> MINERVA
>
> Horace, listen to me, I'm trying to help you understand.

He turns from the window to Minerva.

> HORACE
>
> Oh, I understand. I understand my only

> friend is ditching me for the one mil-
> lionth time, and for what? Some dame he
> just met a few days ago. And she falls
> for him in a big way like all the oth-
> ers. And as usual, I'm left with not
> even so much as a one-eyed librarian
> with a speech impediment this time.

Minerva makes a face and opens her mouth to ask about
the description, Horace turns back to window.

> HORACE
>
> Don't ask.

> MINERVA
>
> This happens all the time?

> HORACE
>
> More often than that. Why if I had a
> nickel for every time he wooed some poor
> skirt into wedding eyes, why I'd have

Counts on both hands, shakes his head in frustration.

> Well, a lot!

Horace goes back to candy window, wide-eyed.

> Whoa! Jawbreakers.

> MINERVA
>
> Why that two-timing little, little

> HORACE
>
> Snake is a fine verb.

> MINERVA
>
> Noun.

> HORACE
>
> Whatever.

Horace goes through his pockets looking for money to
buy candy.

> HORACE
>
> Listen, sister, you look pretty smart to
> me. And, well, you ain't exactly hurtin'
> in the treasury department, so why would
> you want to throw away your independence
> on a ramblin' con man? Suit yourself,

we'll help you and Dusty out, then I'll
blow and you can find out about Sam in
good time.

He finds some change in his pocket, counts it.

Want a lemon drop?

                    MINERVA

You're right, Horace. A little
incoherent, but you're right. What do
I want that for?

                    HORACE

Well, they're better than jawbreakers.

                    MINERVA

Not candy, I mean Sam! What do I want to
get tied down now for? And to a snake-
oil salesman, at that? Oh, he is smooth,
and I nearly fell for it, too.

Pats Horace on the back, nearly knocking him over.

Come on, Horace, tell me more. I'll get
you some lemon drops.

They enter the candy store.

EXT — CANDY STORE - DAY

Minerva and Horace exit the candy store. He has a brown
paper bag in his hand and is stuffing lemon drops into
his mouth.

                    MINERVA

I really want to thank you again,
Horace. I don't know what I would have
done if I'd actually gone with Sam.

                    HORACE

Well, I'd just hate to see you give up
your freedom so early in life.

                    MINERVA

I'll just go tell Sam the deal is off,
set him strait. (resolutely) I don't
need your help, why pay you two to do
something Pop and I can do ourselves?
What a relief.

She slaps Horace on the back again, turns to go back to the Dirty Glass Saloon.

Horace realizes he went too far. Horace stops, his jaw drops, he stares down at his lemon drops.

>   HORACE

> Dang, this is the most expensive candy
> I've ever eaten.

He trots to catch up with Minerva, who walks a few steps in front of him.

Bart steps out from the alleyway into their path, gun aimed at Minerva. Two more FLUNKIES stand behind him.

>   BART

> How-do, miz Minerva? Goin' somewheres?

>   HORACE

> Hey chuckles, why don't you

Another THUG comes up behind Horace and crowns him with a 2 x 4. Horace doesn't even miss a beat, he finishes his sentence.

> go shoot some cans off a fence somewhere,
> or something, Huh?

Horace winces, touches the back of his head, grimaces big.

> OUCH.

He falls to the ground. Bart lowers the gun to aim at Horace.

>   BART

> Not a word, Missie, or I'll put a hole
> in him, too.

Bart gestures with his gun into alley. Minerva looks to Horace, back to Bart, then goes into the alley with the thugs.

Bart flashes a glance up and down the street, then follows.

INT — DIRTY GLASS SALOON — DAY

Horace stumbles into the saloon. Sam and Sticks are at the piano still talking. They see him and jump up.

Shotglass runs to the doors and looks out into street.

                    SHOTGLASS

          I don't see no one.

                       SAM

          That's a double negative, brother. I
          know what you mean, but everybody else
          will think you see someone and,

All three eye him questioningly.

          never mind.

Sam cradles Horace's head in his hands as he crouches.

                       SAM

          Who was it, boy? Where's Minerva?

                      HORACE

          It was Bart, and his pals, they took. ..
          they grabbed... (sobbing) They grabbed
          'em.

                      STICKS

          "Them"? What'd y'all mean "them"? You
          mean Minerva and Dusty?

                      HORACE

          My lemon drops, they took them.

Sam drops Horace's head onto floor with a thunk and runs
out of saloon and looks frantically up and down the
street.

                       SAM

          We've got to help her, Horace. Where did
          they take her?

                      HORACE

          I don't know, I was having an intimate
          conversation with the sidewalk at the
          time.

Shotglass helps Sticks get Horace to his feet.

                    SHOTGLASS

          They probably holed up at the Tanner
          Ranch — it's a couple miles west of
          town.

                      STICKS

          Let's go get 'em!

                    SHOTGLASS

          They's at least ten of 'em, an' they got
          a load 0' guns.

                     STICKS

          Like I said, you boys go git 'em, I'll
          watch the bar.

Sam steps back inside.

                      SAM

          How about it, Shotglass? Can you show us
          how to get there?

                    SHOTGLASS

          I just want to help Minerva. How about
          you, Junior, you okay with that?

                     HORACE

          What do I care if you lose?

                      SAM

          Let's go!

Sticks pours himself a beer at the bar and waves in
their direction.

                     STICKS

          Good Luck, boys.

They scramble out the swinging doors.

INT — TANNER BARN — NIGHT

Minerva is sitting in a chair circled by Bart's
CRONIES. Bart stands across table from her with a
pencil and paper.

                      BART

          Do it, Minerva. Draw the map to the
          gold! If'n you help me, it'll go easier
          on you.

                    MINERVA

          You're wastin' your bad breath on me,
          Tanner. I'll never show you where it is.

                      BART

          I kin play that game, too.

Bart grins and pulls his .45 out for her to see.

                    MINERVA

     You won't do anything to me, or you'll
     never find the gold.

                    BART

     Well, now, honey, thet's true. I won't
     do nothing to you. Conrad.

Bart motions to CONRAD, who grins, and opens a grain
bin door. Inside is Dusty bound and gagged. Conrad
holds a knife to Dusty's throat and grins wider.

                    BART

     How's about if'n I do anything ta yer
     ol' man?

                    MINERVA

     Papa!

Minerva glares at Bart, then at Conrad. She looks to
Dusty, her head lowers.

     (quietly) Okay.

                    BART

     Huh? I kaint hear nuthin'. You hear
     anything, Bordo?

                    BORDO

     Naw, Bart. I didn't hear nuthin'
     neither.

                    BART

     Speak up, honey.

                    MINERVA

     I said ALRIGHT, Bart! I'll draw you a
     map, but you have to let my father go
     first.

                    BART

     Naw sir. You gimmee a map, then I goes
     and gits the loot, then I'll let you go.

                    MINERVA

     How do I know you won't just kill us
     after you get what you want?

                              BART

          You don't. Ha!

The thugs laugh.

               'sides, gold's only haf'n what I want.

Bart leans closer to Minerva's face, licks his lips and
winks.

               Know what I mean?

She grabs paper and pencil from out of Bart's hands.

                            MINERVA

          I'd rather you kill me.

She starts to draw, cronies and Bart laugh, Dusty looks
on from the bin.

EXT — BARN — SAME TIME

Horace, Sam and Shotglass crouch low in the bushes,
they look into a window of barn. Shotglass has a
scattergun.

Horace sits with his back to the barn and his fingers in
his ears, eyes tightly shut, wincing.

                              SAM

          What's it look like to you, can you tell
          how many?

                          SHOTGLASS

          Looks like he's got seven with him,
          maybe more, hard to see. Can't outshoot
          'em, we'll have to come up with a good
          plan.

                              SAM

          Okay, Horace, we need a plan, maybe we
          could.

Sam sees Horace cowering, pulls a finger out of Horace's
ear.

                            HORACE

          Is it over, did we win? Where's Minerva?
          Let's go.

He gets up to leave, Sam and Shotglass pull him back
down with them.

                    SAM

     Hasn't started yet, son. We need a plan.

                    HORACE

     So what are you bothering me for? You
     know in a fight I'm about as useful as a
     two-legged armadillo trying to cross a
     four-lane highway.

Thinks a beat.

     Oh man, I been in Texas too long.

                    SAM

     Quit it, willya. Listen up, Junior.
     Remember Omaha, three years ago?

                    HORACE

     No, remind me.

                    SAM

     We were outnumbered five to one, they
     surrounded us in that boarding house.

Horace starts to feel areas of his torso.

                    HORACE

     Uh, 17 broken ribs and three broken
     ankles?

                    SAM

     That's the one!

                    HORACE

     Yeah, I remember; what happened to you?

                    SAM

     Well, I got the Doctor.

                    HORACE

     Yeah? Is that how you're telling it? You
     went for the doctor a good five minutes
     before they started pounding on me.

                    SAM

     If you're gonna start getting petty
     on me now, Junior, we'll never get
     Minerva out of there. Do you remember
     what we did?

> HORACE
>
> Yes. We got stomped into the floorboards
> while the rest of us ran down the street
> to get Lola Swisher.

> SAM
>
> That's Doctor Swisher.

> HORACE
>
> Yeah, well, just because you two played
> doctor don't make her a surgeon.

> SAM
>
> Now, look, Junior, I had to convince her
> to come help you.

> SHOTGLASS
>
> Hey, I'm thinkin' we should mebbe do
> something,

Sam and Horace glare at each other for a moment or two,
then relax.

> SAM
>
> Shotglass is right, Boy. And Aunt Mar-
> gie would want you to forget that whole
> incident and concentrate on the task at
> hand.

> HORACE
>
> (softens) Aw, alright.

> SAM
>
> Alright. Here's the plan,

Sam trails off.

INT — BARN — SAME TIME

Minerva hands Bart the map. She looks to Dusty, who
smiles weakly and nods. Bart and his buddies laugh.

> BART
>
> Heh heh, thankew, little lady! You
> won't be sorry. With this gold, Little
> 'Dorado's gonna be the biggest little
> city this side of San Francisco.

He waves the map aloft.

> Gamblin', real estate, politikin'. HA!

You 'n' me's gonna be in charge. Yessir,
Little 'Dorado's gonna be famous!

MINERVA

What happened to letting us go?

BART

I didn't say when!

Cronies all laugh.

and what do you mean "us"? Bordo, I say
anything 'bout lettin' the geezer go?

BORDO

Naw, Bart. Just her.

MINERVA

You're a low down good for nothing
skunk, Bart Tanner.

BART

Yeah, I reckon I am, honey, and I got
no use fer a crazy old man, neither.
Conrad! Take him out behind the hog
shed.

Conrad starts to lift Dusty out of the bin. There is a
knock at the barn door. Everyone stops dead, Bart nods
to Bordo and then jerks his head toward the door.

Bordo opens the door and Sam is standing there.

BORDO

It's that other slicker, Bart!

BART

Grab him, he kin keep the old man
company.

MINERVA

Sam! What are you doing here?

SAM

We came to get you and Dusty, there's a
whole posse outside.

He turns to Bart as he slams the door shut.

Bart, we've got a Federal Marshall. You
and your boys are surrounded. You better
let us go.

At a nod from Bart, Bordo opens the door again and
sticks his head out to look around.

                    BORDO

        I don't see no one.

                    SAM

        You're wrong.

                    BORDO

        Why? 'Cause I employed a double
        negative?

                    SAM

        Well, that too. Sam turns his head
        toward the door and shouts. Marshall,
        you guys there?

                    VOICE #1

        We're here, Sam, no one's come Give it
        up, Tanner, we've got you surrounded!

                    BORDO

        What do we do boss?

                    SANTOS

        (in Spanish) <I don't like this.>

Bart flails his arms over his head emphatically.

                    BART

        Shut up! All o' you! Lemme think.

                    SAM

        Just let us go, Bart. Right now it's
        just kidnapping. You don't want to be
        arrested for murder.

                    BART

        (loudly) If'n I let 'em go, you let me
        an' my boys ride on out of here?

                    VOICE #2

        (behind the barn) What'd he say?

                    VOICE #3

        (on the side) He said he'd let them go
        if we let him and the boys ride outta
        town .

                         BORDO

     They're all around us!

                        VOICE #3

     (on side by shuttered window) Alright,
     y'all let the woman and the ol' man go,
     then y'all kin ride outta town. But
     you'd better not show yer face in this
     part of Texas agin!

Bart laughs and waves the map.

                         BART

        You got it.

Bart glances down at the map, clenches it in his fist.
He turns to Minerva and Dusty.

        You heard him, git! Ha ha! Who needs
        you?

                        CONRAD

        Hey, Bart, what about him?

Indicating Sam.

                         BART

     What about the city slicker?

                        VOICE #3

     (still by shutters) Oh, y'all kin do
     what y'all want with him.

Sam makes faces of confusion and incredulity

        Kill him, cook him, eat him for all we
        care.

                         SAM

     Now hold on...

                        VOICE #4

     (falsetto) No, Marshall, don't be so
     callous and unfeeling! Let that good for
     nothing, lying, two-faced, backstabbing,
     sell-his-mother-for-a-buck city slicker
     go.

Bart goes to the window while this is being said, and
opens the shutters.

Horace is standing there making voices, he turns while
he talks until he is face to face with Bart.

                    HORACE AS VOICE #4

        Let him rot I says! He sold me a
        bottle of that oil. Now my spleen is
        all blotchy and irritated.

Sees Bart staring at him.

        Ooh. This is gonna hurt.

                         BART

        Well lookee here, boys. We got us a
        mockin' bird! Heh heh, don't look too
        much like a posse to me. Nawsir.

Grabs Horace by the throat and drags him through the
window and pushes him over by Sam

                         SAM

        "Kill him" you said, "cook him and eat
        him" you said. Why I ought to

                        HORACE

        You ought to what? Walking out on me
        ain't enough for you? You snake, you
        walking slug.

                         SAM

        Why you ingrate! If Aunt Margie were
        here, "take care of him" she said, and
        then she left us.

                        HORACE

        Oh, don't lay that on me anymore. You
        know as well as I do that she left us to
        get a box of cigars and a beer. You're
        the one who snatched me out of a safe
        environment to use me for your own gain.

                         SAM

        Use you? For my own? Oh, that's rich,
        that is really rich.

                         BART

        Shaddap!

He walks quickly over to Sam and Horace.

                    BART

     Save yer breath, you're gonna need it.
     You boys're jest what I need to help
     move thet treasure. I ain't bustin'
     my back.

                   HORACE

     Beg pardon?

                    BART

     What are you, stoopid? I says yer comin'
     with us.

                    SAM

     You heard him, Junior, he said we're
     going with him.

                   HORACE

     We're going with him, huh?

Every time they say "Going with him" they throw a
pointed finger toward Bart for emphasis.

                    SAM

     That's what he said. Going with him.

                   HORACE

     Well then, that's final. Let's go with
     him.

                    SAM

     Let's... go... with... him.

On the last line, they both swing their fists at Bart
knocking him back to the wall, then they turn to knock
down the two flunkies nearest each of them.

They step back a bit so that the wall is at their backs
and they face the angry gang.

A brawl ensues, Sam leaps to the door and opens it wide
just as he is grabbed from behind.

Shotglass enters and starts butting heads with the
stock of his shotgun.

Minerva jumps at Conrad and floors him with one punch.
She grabs his knife, runs to the bin and cuts Dusty's
ropes.

A flunky draws a bead on her with his pistol.

Dusty shouts to warn her. Minerva turns and throws the knife hitting the gunman in the shoulder. He drops the gun and falls.

Minerva hurries Dusty out of the bin and toward the door.

Bart's back is pushed up against Minerva's back. They turn and face each other.

Bart's eyes narrow into slits.

Minerva's eyes narrow into slits.

Bart's eyes widen in fear.

Minerva belts Bart in the stomach.

He doubles over, she grabs the map, upper-cuts Bart and the map is torn in two as he flies across the room into the grain bin.

Minerva and Dusty exit through the door.

Shotglass pummels three cronies with butt of scattergun.

Sam shouts to Horace, Horace ducks just in time to miss chair flying over his head, hitting a lantern, which falls and sets straw on fire.

Horace jumps at Bordo, hitting him in the chest with his head, Bordo goes down.

Sam grabs Horace, Shotglass helps them to their feet as smoke fills the barn.

> SHOTGLASS
>
> I'm thinkin' it's time to leave.

> SAM
>
> I'm thinking the same thing. How about
> you, Junior?

> HORACE
>
> I'm thinking of that time at Coney
> Island when Sam wouldn't let me get
> a snow cone.

> SAM
>
> He's lost it, let's get him outside.

They hustle out the door.

EXT — BARN — NIGHT

Sam, Horace and Shotglass meet up with Dusty and
Minerva.

                    MINERVA

        Sam! Shotglass! Thank God you're
        alright.

                    HORACE

        What about me?

She looks to Horace for a beat or two, then looks back
to the others.

                    MINERVA

        Sam. Shotglass.

                    SHOTGLASS

        We've got horses down by the stream,
        let's get to 'em.

They hurry off in that direction, Horace lags behind.

                    HORACE

        What about me? No thanks that I'm okay?

Sam grabs him by the shoulder and hurries him along

                    SAM

        It's an implied thing, Boy, now let's
        go.

They hustle off toward the stream.

INT — BARN — SAME TIME

Henchmen slap the flames out with saddle blankets, as
Bart looks down and sees the map is ripped in half. He
turns it over a couple times then gives up.

                    BART

        Aaargh! She's got the half with the
        location on it. Git her! Kill them all,
        git that map back.

They all start to move at once, bumping into each
other.

Bart rolls his eyes and pushes men out of the way as
he heads for the horses.

EXT — DOWN BY THE STREAM — NIGHT

Minerva and company get their horses and mount up.

                    MINERVA

     Sam! We've got to get to the cave first
     and seal the entrance.

                     SAM

     How can he find it if you have the map?

                    MINERVA

     I only got half of it, he may have memo-
     rized the location. We have to hide the
     entrance, then we can come back after
     things quiet down.

                    HORACE

     Does this mean we get bupkus?

                    MINERVA

     You can each fill a pocket, that's about
     all we'll have time for.

                     SAM

     We'll help you out for free, Minerva.

                    HORACE

     Yeah, but a small donation to the save
     Sam and Horace fund would be nice.

                    MINERVA

     Shotglass, ride back to town, tell
     everyone that Bart kidnapped Dusty and
     we're being chased to Rattler Creek.

                   SHOTGLASS

     Sure Minerva, good luck.

To Sam and Horace.

     If anybody dies, it'd better be you.

He rides off toward town.

                  SAM AND HORACE

     He talking to you?

                    MINERVA

     Papa, you okay to ride?

                    DUSTY

     Where we going?

MINERVA

Just follow me close. Giddap!

She gallops away followed by Dusty. Sam and Horace just sit atop their horses a moment. They exchange glances.

HORACE

Sam?

SAM

Yeah, Junior?

HORACE

How come we ain't movin'?

Sam looks down at the horses.

SAM

Don't know. (thinks) Oh. (loudly) HYAAA!

Both horses leap into a gallop after Minerva and Dusty.

EXT — BART'S BARN — NIGHT

Bart and gang hurriedly mount horses and ride away.

EXT — DESERT — NIGHT

Minerva and Dusty pull up at the mouth of a small cave.

Sam and Horace come charging to a stop after Dusty and Minerva have dismounted.

HORACE

(winded) Where'd you learn to do that?

SAM

Blekker twins, Knoxville.

HORACE

They didn't have horses.

SAM

Didn't say anything about horses.

Minerva looks up at the darkening sky, the wind is picking up, sand starts to blow.

MINERVA

We'll have to move fast, there's a storm comin' in.

Sam and Horace look at the entrance of the cave, it is fairly large.

                    SAM

     How are we supposed to cover this
     entrance?

                  MINERVA

     There's a load of loose boulders just
     above the mouth. Pop set it up years ago
     just in case something like this ever
     happened. We only have to push a few
     rocks and the whole thing'll come down.

                  HORACE

     If it's all covered up with boulders,
     how do we get paid?

                  MINERVA

     There's a secret entrance around the
     other side of the hill.

Sam whacks Horace upside the head.

                    SAM

     We'll worry about money later, let's get
     this covered up.

They follow Minerva up the slope.

                  MINERVA

     Pop, bring the horses around the side,
     we'll meet you down there in a few min-
     utes.

                  DUSTY

     Right.

A piece of paper drops from Minerva. Horace picks it up and tries to get her attention. She is oblivious and continues on her way.

Horace shrugs and stuffs the paper into his pocket.

Dusty wanders off with the horses in the general direction Minerva indicated. Dust and sand starts to blow harder.

EXT — DESERT — NIGHT

Bart and his gang are stopped. SANTOS is off his horse and checking the trail. The wind gets worse.

                         SANTOS

          Senor Tanner, the tracks are starting
          to get covered up, but I think
          they are heading out toward Rattler
          Creek, I think.

Bart glares out into the desert, he is going around the bend, his mind on one thing only.

                         BART

          Yes, I was right. And they's three caves
          out there in thet dry river bed, we'll
          stop at each one 'til we find 'em.

                         SANTOS

          But the wind, the sand, we should wait
          until the storm passes, I think.

                         BART

          I don't pay you to think, Santos. I'm
          thinking of not paying you at all.

He pulls out his gun and aims it at Santos' head.

          so shut up and ride.

                         SANTOS

          Si, Senor Tanner.

                         BART

          Let's go!

He holsters his pistol and waves his group on, the horses balk at first, but are spurred on.

EXT — CAVE — NIGHT

Minerva and company are on foot leading the horses, the wind is getting so bad they can hardly see through it.

Minerva and Dusty have handkerchiefs tied around their faces.

                         MINERVA

          (shouting over wind) Follow me, boys,
          we'll have to walk the horses from here
          on out. We'll wait out this storm in the
          cave.

                         DUSTY

     I want a lemonade.

Dusty, Sam and Horace follow Minerva, walking the
horses. After a few moments, Minerva and Dusty fade
into the sand.

Sam and Horace panic and try to keep up, but get
tangled in the reins, soon their horses get free and
wander off into the sand.

                         HORACE

     Sam, where'd they go?

                          SAM

     Don't know, Junior, but we'd better find
     some shelter and wait this out. They'll
     find us later.

                         HORACE

     Find our bodies being pecked at by
     vultures most likely.

                          SAM

     Nonsense. Vultures don't peck, they rip,
     and tear with their beaks.

                         HORACE

     At least they don't peck, I hate that.

                          SAM

     Over here, boy, some trees.

They make their way into a clump of trees and bushes,
that break the wind quite a bit. They plop down onto
the ground.

                          SAM

     One good thing about this storm,

                         HORACE

     What's that? We'll suffocate before Bart
     can kill us?

                          SAM

     Nah, no such luck. It means Bart and his
     boys won't be movin' either. Minerva and
     Dusty'll be safe.

                    HORACE

        Yeah, and we'll be the Donner Party.

They gaze through the trees at the storm.

EXT — DESERT — NIGHT

Bart is on horseback, his cronies are afoot and turning
back. Bart yells at them incoherently.

Bart's horse falls. He has the map in one hand as he
falls from his horse and blunders screaming out into
the storm.

INT — CAVE — NIGHT

Minerva and Dusty stand just inside the cave they dust
each other off, she lights lanterns from her saddlebag
and hands one to Dusty.

                    MINERVA

        We made it, Pop! We'll wait out the
        storm here. Shotglass and the others
        won't be out tonight in this. Then we'll
        pack up and, where are they?

                    DUSTY

        Who?

                    MINERVA

        Sam and Horace. They were right behind
        us!

                    DUSTY

        Those city boys? I like them.

Minerva stares out into the night

                    MINERVA

        So do I, Pop, so do I.

She shakes her head frantically.

        We've got to go after them, Pop. We
        can't leave them to die, we have to go
        back for them. We HAVE TO!

                    DUSTY

        They're probably already gone.

                    MINERVA

        Okay. Nevermind.

She stares out into the sand for awhile as Dusty
wanders off. Soon he calls to her.

                    DUSTY

    Minerva! Lookie this!

Minerva comes out of her trance and hurries to see what
it is.

INT — ANOTHER CAVE ROOM — NIGHT

Minerva comes up behind Dusty and looks over his
shoulder.

The small cavern is filled with chests of gold, jewels
and artifacts. It seems to glow from its own light, the
lantern makes it even more brilliant.

                    MINERVA

    We're safe now.

                    DUSTY

    This what we been lookin' fer? All this
    junk?

                    MINERVA

    Huh?

                    DUSTY

    All this junk, is this what you been
    talkin' about all this time?

                    MINERVA

    Yeah, Pop. We're gonna leave Little
    Dorado and start a new life.

                    DUSTY

    Hog feathers! The only treasure I need
    is you, and the memory of your mother.
    The hell with this, Tanner can have it.

                    MINERVA

    Are you sure? Are you ...

                    DUSTY

    Crazy again? Shucks, Honey, don't take
    a crazy person to see that this is just
    stuff, won't never take the place a' you.

MINERVA

Whatever you say Papa.

She gives him a huge hug and a kiss, they turn and leave. Dusty stops a few feet away.

DUSTY

Where you goin', Minerva?

MINERVA

Leavin', like you said.

DUSTY

I may me going senile, girl, but I ain't stupid. Grab a hunk o' that junk; we got to live on something.

Minerva laughs and starts to fill a set of saddlebags on the floor.

EXT — DESERT — DAY

Sam and Horace lay curled up on the ground facing each other. Sam awakens, sits up and dusts himself off, he looks around.

SAM

Horace, Horace wake up, the storm's passed.

HORACE

(dreaming, smiles and giggles) In a minute, Gretchen, you make breakfast this time, I'm still sore from that spatula.

SAM

(nudges him) C'mon, Junior, we've got to get going and find Minerva and Dusty.

HORACE

(takes Sam's hand) Ooh, you're feisty today.

Horace kisses Sam's hand, giggles.

there, that's all you get for now.

Sam smacks him in the head.

SAM

Wake up, you babbling fool.

                    HORACE

     (jumps up) Mom?

                     SAM

     It's me, Sam. Look, the storms over, we
     can pick up their trail to the cave now.

Looks down at sand.

     Hmmm,

Horace rubs his eyes and sits up.

                    HORACE

     I know that "Hmmm," Sam. That's NOT an
     "Oh, here's the trail" Hmmm; that's a
     "Oh, Hell, what do we do now" sort of
     Hmmm,

                     SAM

     Now, don't panic, boy. I'm sure we can
     still find them. We'll just go in the
     direction we were headed last night,
     around the other side of the Junior, it
     isn't that bad.

                    HORACE

     "We'll help you for free" you said; "No"
     I said; "Shut up and follow me" you
     said; "I wanna get paid" I said.

                     SAM

     What good would gold do us now? We'd
     just have to lug it all around.

                    HORACE

     Gold ain't heavy, it just feels that
     way.

Horace hangs his head into his hands and pouts.
                     SAM

     C'mon, we'll go. Which way do you think
     we should go?

                    HORACE

     Since when do you care what I think?

                    SAM

     There you go again with the selfish
     attitude. I try to let you be a part of
     the decision making process, and all you
     can do is doubt my sincerity.

                  HORACE

      Well, gee, Sam, I didn't

                    SAM

     A simple question, I ask you a simple
     question — deferring to your judgment,
     mind you — and you bite my head off.
     I got us into this mess, and all I ask
     is you to tell us which way to get out
     of it.

                  HORACE

     We should go that way.

He points off to the RIGHT.

                    SAM

     You sure?

                  HORACE

     Positive.

                    SAM

     Certain?

                  HORACE

     I've never been more certain of anything
     in my whole life. I would go that way.

                    SAM

     Alright, let's go.

Sam heads off to the LEFT, Horace follows.

EXT — DESERT — DAY

Sam and Horace trudge through desert, sun blazes down
on them. Horace slips and falls, Sam helps him up.

Sam plods wearily in and out of frame, he has his shirt
on his head to protect him from the sun.

A beat passes, then Horace follows the same direction,
he has his pants on his head.

Sam stops by a log, looking around to get his bearings.
Horace plops down on the log next to him.

                    HORACE

        I'm tired, I'm hungry, I'm

                    SAM

        Annoying.

                    HORACE

        Is that something you get from being out
        in the desert for hours and hours?

                    SAM

        You do.

                    HORACE

        Then I'm annoying, too. Heck, I'd settle
        for a broom closet at this point

Sam sighs and sits next to Horace.

                    SAM

        I can't even find Little 'Dorado again.
        I'm sorry, boy. I guess we're just plain
        lost. We might as well plan on spending
        the night right here.

He starts to go through his pockets.

        Let's see if we've got anything to eat
        in our pockets.

They fumble through their pockets. Sam produces a
watch, a pencil and a piece of paper.

Horace take out a comb, a frog, a piece of paper, half
a bra and a boot spur.

Sam looks at the bra half and spur, then to Horace.

                    HORACE

        What?

                    SAM

        I'm not even gonna ask. Hey, what's
        that?

He indicates the piece of paper Horace has. It is white
and wrinkled.

                    HORACE

     It's that piece of map Minerva took from
     Bart. She dropped it at the cave. I
     guess I forgot to give it back.

                     SAM

     Look.

He shows his piece of paper, the one he got from the
cave near the beginning, it is yellowed and wrinkled.

                     SAM

     It looks like it fits the one we found on
     that skeleton a few days ago.

They look at each other.

                    HORACE

     Put them together!

                     SAM

     Here, hold yours up, whoa!

They hold up the pieces and see the rips match up.

                    HORACE

     Sam! It's the whole map:

                     SAM

     And look! This big boulder here, it'
     right over there. This hill here is that
     hill right over there. That means that,

A gust of wind blows the map halves away. Sam goes
after one of them, indicates the other to Horace.

                     SAM

     Junior, grab that half!

                    HORACE

     You get that one!

They chase the pieces for a few moments until Sam loses
his and stops and just stares after it as it blows way
out of reach.

Horace chases his up to Sam, than leaps at it and lands
on his face in a cloud of dust. He looks up and sees
his piece blowing away in the opposite direction.

Sam sighs and slaps his thighs.

                         SAM

          Looks like we made it back, Junior. It's
          all gone now, everything.

                       HORACE

          That's it. Sam, I can't take it anymore.

                         SAM

          What's with you, boy? We've lost
          fortunes before.

                       HORACE

          It's too much, I can't stand it, ha ha
          ha, it's driving me mad. Mad I tell you,
          ha ha ha ha. The sun. The wind. The sun,
          the gold the sand, did I mention the
          sun? The heat! I can't handle it, Sam.
          Put me out of my misery, put me out of
          my misery.

Horace is on his knees shaking his fists at the sky, his
head thrown back.

Sam stands by waiting for him to finish.

A tour BUS pulls to a stop behind them on the road they
were just ten feet from.

Sam and Horace look back at the bus, then to each
other. Horace stands, indignant.

                       HORACE

          Oh, give me a break.

Door of the bus opens to show DRIVER.

                       DRIVER

          You boys need a lift? Shouldn't be out
          in this sun with no water.

Sam and Horace just stare, then they shrug and get
aboard the bus.

INT — BUS — IMMEDIATELY FOLLOWING

                         SAM

          We appreciate it, Pop.

                       HORACE

          Yeah, thanks.

They see there is no one else on the bus, so they find
seats near the front and sink into them.

> DRIVER

Ya'll kin get tickets when we get to the
next stop. Where to?

> HORACE

Ah, who cares? Just drive.

> DRIVER

You got it.

The driver smiles and adjusts a knob over his head.

EXT — BUS WINDSHIELD — FOLLOWING

The "charter" sign in the front window of the bus flips
to read "Atlantis." The bus pulls out, and we follow it
as it speeds away into the desert.

FADE OUT

THE END

KOPY KINGS
a comedy by class clown pictures
WINNER
Carrboro
Film Festival
FILM EXCELLENCE
2016
OFFICIAL SELECTION
FROSTBITE
International Film
Festival
2017
WINNER
Windy City
International Film
Festival
INDIE SPIRIT AWARD
2017
BEST COMEDY
Alaska
International Film
Awards
2017
WINNER
BEST of the FEST
AUSTIN
INDIE FEST
2017
AUDIENCE CHOICE
MOTION for
PICTURES
screening series
FEBRUARY 2018
Error
BORN TO COPY
Saving the World...
one copy at a time.
CLASS CLOWN PICTURES PRESENTS "KOPY KINGS" KIRA POZEHL DAVID MOXHAM DARRELL MITCHELL
JOE BUNNER PATRICK GROVER WITH DAVID BLACKWELL MUSIC BY BILLY MUTSCHLER DIRECTOR OF PHOTOGRAPHY ERIC GRAHAM
EXECUTIVE PRODUCER CARMEN ZAYAS PRODUCED BY GREG DORCHAK WRITTEN AND DIRECTED BY GREG DORCHAK

KOPY KINGS

Most of my adult life was spent working for publications and print shops, starting with working at the 24-hour Kinko's across the street from the University of Nevada Las Vegas in the mid 80s. It was quite an experience, the interesting ==types of folks that came in at 2am, not to mention the sort of people that worked there.

With every subsequent print shop I worked at, the cache of characters built up, as did the situations and interactions. So when I got around to writing my third script, it was a no-brainer for me – I mean, "write what you know" and whatnot, right?

The theme that ran through the story was pretty easy to grasp as well, I told the basic story of how my wife and I met, though I changed the setting from a student newspaper to a print shop instead – in my head it felt easier to make a movie in a print shop than a newspaper office, even if I wasn't going to make the movie myself.

The story in *Kopy Kings*, the people, the interactions, etc., are an amalgam of everybody I ever met, worked with, or dealt with over (at that point) the last 15 years. It was set in Las Vegas and was originally called *Moxie's*. It was a lot of fun to write, and it did pretty well at every screenplay competition I sent it to, nabbing a handful of runner-up, finalist, and first place awards.

When I started to think seriously about producing and directing movies myself, *Kopy Kings* was there, jumping up and down in my head yelling "Pick Me PICK ME." I dusted it off, and took a long look at it again, and realized it was in need of an overhaul. Biggest issue was I no longer lived in Las Vegas, having called Austin home for about ten years at that point. Austin had the same vibe though, so making that transition was pretty smooth.

However, another movie opportunity dropped in my lap, and I had to pursue it. I wrote it with another film maker – something I hated, but the script was solid – and the production had grown legs and we went for it.

It ended up crashing and burning in epic proportions, right at the start of the Market Crash in 2008, and we got SQUASHED. HARD.

Seven years later, in February, while scouting locations to get that crashed project up and running again, we passed a print shop that had been closed for a few years... but now the lights were on. We pulled in, found the owners on site, and one owner thought the idea of making a movie in their shop was the coolest thing ever.

My wife and I went home, ran some numbers, made a list of pros and cons... and we decided we could make this movie. By September of that year, cameras rolled on *Kopy Kings* in North Austin, and we had a ton of fun making it into a movie.

So if you get a chance, you can find the movie on streaming platforms; but for now, I think the story is a hoot to read as well.

FADE IN:

INT — PRINTSHOP PRODUCTION ROOM — NIGHT

MAGGIE McCALLISTER — 30's, smart, too much on her
mind — stands catatonic at a counter collating PAPERS
together by hand. The PHONE next to her rings, she
comes out of her stupor and answers.

> MAGGIE

Thank you for calling Kopy King Down-
town, we're open 24 hours; this is
Maggie, how can I...

She continues to collate while she talks.

> MAGGIE

Hey Dan. Working. You? (pause) Yeah,
the new guy's here, he's working in
bindery with Stephanie. (beat) So far
so good, why?

She gets an annoyed look on her face.

> MAGGIE

I know a thing or two about hiring...
you can huh? Just by looking at him?
(pause) Yeah, well who cares what you
think — you're the ONLY one who knows

> anything, right? Dan Sommers, saving the
> world one copy at a time.

There is a COMMOTION somewhere off camera, Maggie
doesn't tune in. It's LOUD.

> MAGGIE
>
> Says you. (pause) Yeah well, we'll see.
> I think I'm a pretty good judge of char-
> acter, and I can hire... and train...
> if not better as you can... with the
> damn... what the HELL

She is distracted by the noise, LOUDER now, and
complicated by people YELLING and calling for help.

A cloud of black SMOKE wafts toward Maggie. Some bright
flashes burst from OS. In the background, another
employee dashes to the FIRST AID KIT on the wall, rips
it off and runs back.

Maggie glances in the direction of the runner, does a
double take, stops collating and hangs her head. She
then continues to collate and talk on the phone.

> MAGGIE
>
> Hey Dan, just asking; is the fire extin-
> guisher charged? (pause) No... reason...

INT — MAGGIE'S OFFICE — DAY

Maggie sits at her desk with an open folder in front of
her.

She holds an employment application and addresses SALLY
sitting across from her.

> MAGGIE
>
> Have you ever worked in a print — shop
> or copy center before?

> SALLY
>
> No. But I made a lot of copies in our
> office at my last job. How much different
> can this be?

INT — PRINTSHOP PRODUCTION ROOM — NIGHT

SALLY is at a high-speed copier. She waves her finger
over the control panel, thinking, then presses a
button.

A strobe flashes in the machine, copies come out in the

top tray in a neat stack. SALLY smiles proudly and
turns to a book she's binding.

> SALLY

> You got this, girl.

Behind her, the tray jams, paper spews out onto the
copier and floor at an incredible rate. The strobe goes
faster, the machine shakes and smokes.

She turns and panics. She can't stop the copier or
clear the jammed paper to keep the flow going. Paper
everywhere. She freaks.

> SALLY

> Oh for the love of Christ...

INT — MAGGIE'S OFFICE — DAY

DON, a huge, sweaty, pony-tailed man in a nice suit
sits in front of Maggie. She looks him over. He fidgets
and smiles WAY too genially.

> MAGGIE

> So, Don. Have you ever worked a counter,
> or been in a job where you dealt with
> customers' needs?

> DON

> Yes, many times, as it says on my
> resume. I've worked at Macdonald's,
> Payless Shoes, JC Penney, Fry's and
> Jamba Juice. I think you'll find I deal
> exceptionally well with customers.

INT — PRINTSHOP PRODUCTION ROOM — DAY

Don is with a SILENT MAN at the counter. The
customer's non-committal face changes ever so slightly
as they interact.

> DON

> Welcome to Kopy King, what can I do for
> you, sir?

The silent man sets a stack of papers down on the
counter, points to a copy, starts to open his mouth.

> DON

> Oh, I see what you mean, it's just a
> small fleck.

The silent man looks up at Don. No change in his demeanor whatsoever.

> DON
>
> Okay, okay, I'll take care of it. Please don't take that attitude with me, sir.

The silent man lightly purses his lips. Don wigs.

> DON
>
> What is your problem, man? It's one little smudge. The entire rest of the order is spotless. What are you, some sort of bean-counting neo-fascist Big-Brother anal boy? Why are you persecuting me?

The silent man stares blankly at Don and puts his fingertips gently on the counter in front of him.

Don backs up a step and shoots both hands up, palms out toward the man.

> DON
>
> Back off, storm trooper. This kind of Type-A combativeness may work in LA, but Don Carter's momma didn't raise no door mat; so you can take your over-achieving Bolshevik ass out of my store.

Silent Man thinks a bit as his gaze wanders slowly from Don's face to the counter, then back up. Don sprints for the back office, hands flailing.

> DON
>
> Somebody call the cops!

INT — MAGGIE'S OFFICE — DAY

Maggie slumps lower at her desk.

A KID with piercings and gauges stares at her with a stupid grin. He has about a dozen piercings in his face.

> MAGGIE
>
> Are you good with your hands; like with manual labor, folding, collating, that sort of thing?

> PIERCINGS KID
>
> Dude. I did eight of these piercings myself.

INT — PRODUCTION ROOM — NIGHT

The Piercings Kid uses a sorting machine. It jams. He sticks his head in close to investigate, one of his ear gauges gets snagged. He flails about.

PIERCINGS KID

Dude, what the Hell? OW OW OWWW

INT — MAGGIE'S OFFICE — DAY

Maggie mashes her face with her hand as she looks through more resumes.

Series of shots

A MAN with a BABY sits across from Maggie.

BABY MAN

Can I bring my kid to work three days a week? He is SOOO quiet.

A PROFESSIONAL WOMAN in a business suit.

PROFESSIONAL WOMAN

I'll need at least 55K to start. And an expense account. Is there assigned park-ing?

A BOY with a vacuous stare.

VACUOUS BOY

My mom made me apply.

A GIRL with green hair and a sour face.

PEOPLE HATING GIRL

I want to work graveyard shift because I really freaking hate people.

A WOMAN with too much makeup.

MAKEUP WOMAN

You're serious? You make copies? Of, like... what?

End of series

INT — PRINTSHOP PRODUCTION ROOM — DAY

Maggie drags herself out into the production room, an open area with windows that look out into the street.

The space behind the counter is crammed with production equipment and cluttered countertops.

EMPLOYEES wearing aprons with the Kopy King logo go about their jobs.

DAN SOMMERS — 30's, intelligent offspring of a cuddly grizzly and a mule — is working on the cutter.

                    DAN

          How's it going on that last hire,
          Maggie?

Maggie shuffles over and stares at him.

                    DAN

          Come on, you're making this tougher than
          it needs to be.

                    MAGGIE

          Dan, my last interview wanted to know
          what kind of crystals we use so that she
          could tune hers in when she comes to
          work.

                    DAN

          A: Don't make fun of what you don't
          understand, and B: she could help bring
          in work from the ever-important Proto-
          plasmic Entity demographic.

He readjusts the paper he's cutting.

                    DAN

          You promised. One last interview, then I
          take over.

                    MAGGIE

          Ok, you win, Dan. If I can't hire any-
          one by the end of the day, I'll give it
          up.

                    DAN

          Ooh, baby. About time.

                    MAGGIE

          No, I mean I'll let you do it ...you can
          fill the opening...

                    DAN

          Keep talking like that and I'll make you
          buy me a drink.

Maggie catches herself, stops and takes a breath.

                    MAGGIE

          Do you have to make everything sound
          like a filthy come-on?

                    DAN

          No. You're doing pretty good on your
          own.

                    MAGGIE

          You know what I mean.

Dan laughs evilly, wrings his hands, then presses a
button. The blade comes down on a stack of paper with
a thunk.

                    DAN

          My plan is working perfectly.

Maggie walks away to the front counter, where a
disgruntled customer, JERRY, is arguing with FINNY —
wise-ass spaz — about his order.

MIKE — 40-50's, laid-back hippie — is half hidden
behind the bindery counter. He shouts up to Finny.

                    MIKE

          You need some help there, Finny?

                    FINNY

          No! I'm fine.

Mike turns off the noisy folder and starts to make his
way around his counter.

                    MIKE

          Sure? I can explain that...

Finny turns and motions to Mike, stopping him dead.

                    FINNY

          No, please, I can handle this, just
          finish your job.

Mike shrugs and turns the folder back on.

Maggie directs her attention to Finny and Jerry.

                    JERRY

          It's the wrong size. I asked you to copy

> it at 100 percent and you reduced it.
> I saw you.

>> FINNY

> Yeah, but, reducing it...

>> JERRY

> Ha! You admit it. I KNEW it.

>> FINNY

> What are you, twelve?

Maggie steps up and lets Finny back off.

>> MAGGIE

> Afternoon, Jerry. What's the issue
> today?

>> JERRY

> This guy didn't do what I asked, then
> he lied to me.

>> MAGGIE

> I'm sure none of my employees lie,
> Jerry.

>> JERRY

> I asked him to copy this at a hundred
> percent, and he didn't follow my in-
> struction, then he told me...

>> FINNY

> You know who else doesn't follow
> instructions well? Your mother...
> every night...

>> MAGGIE

> Finny, finish that two o'clock padding
> job, please.

Finny turns to the padding machine behind them.

>> MAGGIE

> Jerry, why do you have to be like this
> every time?

>> JERRY

> DOCTOR Wegner...

                    MAGGIE

        Really, Jerry? We made copies of your
        transcripts. You didn't quite finish
        that online program, did you? Nevermind
        "Doctor."

Jerry looks down, mumbles incoherently.

                    MAGGIE

        And we've had this conversation before,
        Jerry. Because of the nature of the
        process, older photostatic copiers like
        these tend to normally enlarge images
        about two percent, so in order to keep
        your work at the same size, we have to
        compensate by reducing two percent to
        ninety eight percent, that keeps it at a
        hundred percent. Can you follow that...
        DOCTOR?

Jerry scrunches up his brow, tries to answer. The two
stare at each other a beat.

                    MAGGIE

        No charge?

                    JERRY

        Thank you.

He holds the original and copy up to the light and
leaves.

DARLA — 20's, goofy, rough-around-the-edges — brings a
boxed job to the counter, slaps a label on it.

                    MAGGIE

        Saving the world, one copy at a time.

                    DARLA

        Huh?

                    MAGGIE

        Nothing.

Dan squeezes past Maggie and Darla with a big box of
coil-bound books.

                    DAN

        Didn't we just spray for Jerry last
        week? TechTown catalogs are done. They

>   need to go out afternoon delivery,
>   Darla, schedule that, yeah?

                    DARLA

>   Roger that Blue Leader.

Mike turns off the folder, picks up his boxed pages and
starts to move toward them.

                    MIKE

>   Maggie, Live Oak Baptist Church is ready
>   to be collated, I'll bring them up...

Maggie, Dan and Finny look to the customers in the
store, then all turn at the same time.

                    MAGGIE/DAN/FINNY

>   No!

                    MIKE

>   It's no big deal, I don't mind.

He continues to move, the three get more emphatic

                    MAGGIE

>   Please just set them down, Mike we'll
>   come get them.

                    DAN

>   Leave them right there.

                    FINNY

>   For the love of God and all that is
>   holy, put the job down.

Mike shrugs, puts the boxes down, puts up his hands and
backs away to his station making a mock-fear face.

The three sigh in relief and turn away. Finny and Dan
look at Maggie.

                    DAN

>   I didn't hire him.

INT — PRINTSHOP PRODUCTION ROOM — DAY

Maggie and Finny are collating pages together at the
counter.

BRAD MANN — late 20's-30s, pretty-boy fratty guy —
enters the store. He approaches Finny.

                    BRAD

          Excuse me, I'm Brad Mann. I have an
          appointment with Maggie McCallister
          at three.

Finny gives him the once over and jerks his head toward
Maggie.

                    FINNY

          That's her. Knock yourself out.

Maggie looks up and does a double take.

                    MAGGIE

     Hi

                    BRAD

     Hi

There is an awkward silence as Maggie loses her brain
for a few seconds.

                    BRAD

     I have an appointment with you?

                    MAGGIE

     Oh? Oh, yes. Sorry, I ...

                    FINNY

     ...forgot to take my medication.

                    MAGGIE

     Shut up, Finny. Um, okay, back here.

She motions for him to come around the counter.

                    BRAD

       Thank you.

He follows her and together they go toward the back.

ANTOINETTE DUQUESNE — 30-40, very classy — walks up to
the counter with a box and drops it down in front of
Finny. She has a heavy French accent.

                    ANTOINETTE

          Excuse me, I pick this up yesterday and
          when I get it home, I notice a problem.

                    FINNY

     Uh ...okaaaaay.

INT — MAGGIE'S OFFICE — DAY

Maggie pulls a chair for Brad, then seats herself. She takes out a file and opens it on her desk, sneaking another peek at Brad as she does so.

                    MAGGIE

        Well, you look pretty good.

                    BRAD

        Excuse me?

                    MAGGIE

        On your resume ...your resume looks
        good, not you. I mean you look good on
        my desk. Your resume...

                    BRAD

        I think I understand, don't go any
        further.

                    MAGGIE

        Let me start over. My name's Maggie.

                    BRAD

        Hi. Brad Mann.

                    MAGGIE

        You've already spoken with Jane over
        in HR?

                    BRAD

        Yes. She said you needed more people
        at this branch.

                    MAGGIE

        Right. You, um, don't really seem to
        have any experience with...

Brad leans in close.

                    BRAD

        You look like a smart woman, can we
        speak frankly?

                    MAGGIE

        Please. I suck at interviewing.

                    BRAD

        I, uh, I really need a job. I don't have

a lot of experience in print shops, no.
I've lived on a farm in Oklahoma most of
my life. My parents recently died, and I
lost the farm in a flood. I need the work
so I can finish my degree.

                    MAGGIE

I'm really sorry, about your parents.
What made you move to Austin?

                    BRAD

I have a sister here. Anyway, I'm going
to school at UT. Getting my degree so I
can keep a promise to Mom and Pop.

                    MAGGIE

Wow. Uh, so, you need a flexible schedule, insurance.

                    BRAD

Oh, man, if only we could have had
insurance when Ma was sick. She had
the cancer.

She slaps the folder closed.

                    MAGGIE

You're hired. There. That was easy. I
hate that bullshit where you have to try
to impress people to make this place
look more exciting than it is. Eleven
bucks an hour sound cool?

                    BRAD

Sure.

                    MAGGIE

We'll get your paperwork and schedule
figured out later. Let me give you a tour
right quick. Can you start Monday?

                    BRAD

Gosh, sure. Thank you, ma'am.

                    MAGGIE

Ma'am? Maggie. Come on, I'll introduce
you around.

She gets up and opens the door. Brad exits and she follows.

INT — PRINTSHOP PRODUCTION ROOM — DAY

Antoinette is nearly yelling at Finny, who just stares at her with a half grin.

> ANTOINETTE
>
> Well? What are you going to do about this?

> FINNY
>
> Um, I will personally take care of this, Ms... Ms...?

> ANTOINETTE
>
> Duquesne.

> FINNY
>
> Alright, Ms. Duquesne. We'll fix the mistake and it'll be done tomorrow morning. How's that?

> ANTOINETTE
>
> Oh. Okay. Thank you,

She peers at Finny's name tag.

> ANTOINETTE
>
> Stuart.

She composes herself, turns and leaves. Darla draws close to Finny.

> DARLA
>
> Damn. That woman ripped you up and down.

> FINNY
>
> Yeah. Ain't she sexy?

> DARLA
>
> You're disturbed, Finny.

Darla shakes her head, and walks away.

Maggie and Brad walk over to Finny.

> MAGGIE
>
> Finny, you met Brad, he'll be starting on Monday.

Brad and Finny shake hands, Finny hardly notices him.

                    BRAD

     Hi. Brad Mann

                    FINNY

     Yep. Yep. Yep.

He takes the job back to Mike's area. Darla smiles like
a horny teenager and extends her hand.

                    DARLA

      Hi, Brad. Darla. If you need anything...

Maggie swiftly moves him toward another area.

                    MAGGIE

     Darla.

                    BRAD

     She seems real nice.

                    MAGGIE

     Yes, she is. You can't even see her
     prison tatts in that blouse. Over here
     is Dan, my Assistant Manager. Dan?

Dan turns, grinning, from the copier. It is open and
parts of it are pulled out. His grin fades as he looks
Brad over.

                    MAGGIE

     This is Brad. He starts Monday.

Dan looks at Maggie, who keeps gawking at Brad, then
back to Brad. He half smiles, nods at his hands, does
not shake.

Maggie watches as silence ensues.

                    MAGGIE

     Dan means that he's glad you're here to
     help lessen the work load.

                    DAN

     Yeah. That.

Brad smiles and indicates the copier.

                    BRAD

     Wow, wouldn't even know where to begin.

Dan stares at Maggie.

                    DAN

          Yeah. Well, I'm sure you'll try to figure
          it out.

Maggie tears her eyes away from Brad and tries to look
innocent. Brad has a brain fart.

                    BRAD

          Well, I ... bet that... um...

                    MAGGIE

          Dan'll train you. You can shadow some of
          the others, too.

Maggie hurries Brad away as Dan mouths the word "nice"
to her, then turns back to his work.

                    MAGGIE

          Dan's the best, don't know what I'd do
          without him.

                    BRAD

          Less speaking on his part, from the
          looks of it.

                    MAGGIE

          Oh, he's okay, that old machine is a
          pain in the ass, breaks down a lot.

BARRY — 40's tall, thin, well-dressed effeminate man —
walks from the back tying his apron.

                    BARRY

          Maggie, those invites for the Peterson's
          came back last night.

                    MAGGIE

          They didn't like them.

                    BARRY

          Sure didn't. Ugly-ass color she picked
          out. They changed to the burgundy, like
          I suggested the first time.

                    MAGGIE

          Barry, this is Brad Mann, he is starting
          on...

Barry extends his hand, very lady-like to Brad.

126

                    BARRY

     Brad MAN. Mmm-mm. You certainly are.

                    MAGGIE

     Barry is our special orders consultant.

                    BARRY

     Any special orders you'd like to give
     me, Mister Maaannn?

                    MAGGIE

     Down, Barry.

                    BARRY

     Awww. I'm just messing with him.

Brad just stares. Barry winks at him.

                    BRAD

     O...kay.

                    MAGGIE

     Barry does a Drag show.

                    BARRY

     Good to meet you, Bradley. Come on down
     Friday and check out my show.

Barry scoots over to his desk and sits.

                    BRAD

     He's a little... out-going.

                    MAGGIE

     Yeah. Like the Germans in Poland.

Brad notices Mike working on the folding machine.

                    BRAD

     Who's that?

                    MAGGIE

     That's Mike. Let's go get you a hand-
     book.

                    BRAD

     Shouldn't I meet him?

                    MAGGIE

     Nope. Handbook.

She about-faces him quickly, heads back to the counter.
Dan eyes them.

As Brad follows her we catch a glimpse of Mike from
behind. He isn't wearing any PANTS. At all.

EXT — KOPY KING'S PARKING AREA — NIGHT

Dan takes jumper cables from under the hoods of his and
Maggie's cars.

> DAN
>
> So... pretty boy, huh?

> MAGGIE
>
> You mean Brad?

> DAN
>
> No, I mean Mike. Of course I mean Brad.
> Does he know how to tie his own shoes?
> Is he familiar with the concept of
> "shoe?"

> MAGGIE
>
> He's off the farm. He's working on his
> degree.

> DAN
>
> A: Five bucks says that weenie never
> worked a day in his life. And B: if he
> did, it sure as hell wasn't on any farm.

> MAGGIE
>
> Come on Dan...

Dan holds up a hand, it is stained, with cuts and
scratches.

> DAN
>
> I'm a writer. I sit on my ass ten hours
> a day tapping keys and my hands look
> like this.

> MAGGIE
>
> Yeah but you work here too.

> DAN
>
> Uh-huh. You ever work on a farm? It's
> more than eight or ten hours. That guy
> hasn't got a single callous, scar or...

                    MAGGIE

     For someone who can't even say hello,
     you sure checked him out a lot.

                     DAN

     (beat) Not as much as you did.

                    MAGGIE

     Excuse me?

                     DAN

     I thought you were gonna strain a cornea
     ogling him.

                    MAGGIE

     Oh, please. NOT my type.

                     DAN

     Really? You have a type? Enlighten me.

                    MAGGIE

     (perturbed) I'll let you know when it's
     any of your damn business.

Finny and Darla exit the store, Finny points and laughs
loudly like an idiot.

                    FINNY

     Ha ha... Dan's jumping Maggie...
     hahahaha

                    DARLA

     Whoooooo!

Dan and Maggie just give him a look, then look back
at each other; she gets in her car and starts to pull
away.

                    MAGGIE

     Grow up, Finny. (to Dan, terse) Thanks.

                     DAN

     That went well.

INT — PRINTSHOP PRODUCTION ROOM — NIGHT

Dan enters the back door, sees a MAN and WOMAN at the
counter with three huge boxes of papers.

STEPHANIE — any age, neat and professional — is helping
them.

CICI, another second-shifter, is aggravated as she works on the laminater.

                    DAN

     Hey Cici, just came in to grab a job I
     sent from home.

                    CICI

     It's on the counter. Have you worked
     with that idiot Don yet? This woman left
     us a bunch of photos of her kids to copy
     at different sizes and then laminate, and
     he does this.

She holds up a long sheet of plastic with all the
original photos laminated with note tags still covering
them.

                    DAN

     And?

                    CICI

     Jesus. That guy. Dan, we need a new new
     guy. He ruins everything he touches. Can
     we get him a prescription for Spazzinol?

                    DAN

     I'll see what I can do. Put this in the
     office, I'll call her.

                    STEPHANIE

     Dan, you got a minute?

                    DAN

     Sure, what's up?

                    STEPHANIE

     These folks are from Wortner and Girten,
     Accountants. They have three boxes of
     receipts, forms and documents that they
     need six copies of by next week.

Dan looks the boxes over.

                    DAN

     Single sided, all black and white? Any
     staples or paper clips?

                    WG MAN

    Yes, all black and white. Maybe some
    staples and a few paper clips. A lot of
    receipts, and invoices and the like.

                     DAN

    Stephanie told you it's extra to unsta-
    ple and clip things back together?

                   WG WOMAN

    Yes. We were just concerned, because of
    the nature of these files.

                    WG MAN

    Concerned.

                   WG WOMAN

    Confidential.

                    WG MAN

    Highly confidential.

                     DAN

    I understand. No one will read any of
    this material or be careless in any way.

                    WG MAN

    We don't mean to imply anything. It's
    just very important that they take extra
    care.

                   WG WOMAN

    VERY sensitive documents.

                     DAN

      It's in the best of hands. Our graveyard
      shift is very discreet and professional.

INT — PRINTSHOP PRODUCTION ROOM — NIGHT

SARAH — late 20's, an air of extreme confidence, and
PIP — 20s, question authority type — sit on the counter
reading pages from the accountants' boxes. Wine cooler
bottles and snack wrappers litter the area.

They laugh hysterically.

                    SARAH

      Check this out, man. She's paying this
      guy a grand a month to "clean the pool."

> PIP
>
> Wonder what else he's cleaning. Holy
> crap! These clowns are buying up the
> whole East Side! fuckin' gentrification,
> man.

> SARAH
>
> Look at these contracts... they are
> giving away half the city...

Pip reaches for his drink but spills it on a stack of
papers.

> SARAH
>
> Oh man, that can't be good.

They just stare for a beat or two.

> SARAH
>
> Throw it away, they'll never read half
> this shit.

Pip wads it up and shoots across the room into a trash
can.

> PIP
>
> Two points!

Two YOUNG WOMEN — sorority girls — enter and go to the
counter in front of Sarah.

> GIRL ONE
>
> Hi, we're from the Delta Kappa Phi Lit-
> tle Sisters. We need to make some flyers.
> How much are the really bright papers?

Sarah looks up and stares. Is this a real thing?

> GIRL TWO
>
> Hello? We need flyers. And we're on a
> budget. We were told we could get a re-
> ally good deal here. At night.

> SARAH
>
> Says who?

> GIRL ONE
>
> Our friend. Alice.

> SARAH
>
> Pip?

                    PIP

     Yeah?

                  SARAH

     Delta Kappa Phi Little Sisters. Say
     Alice sent them.

Pip looks them up and down.

                    PIP

     What do you need?

                 GIRL TWO

     We need as many of these posters as we
     can get on "Greengo Star" or "Orange-
     Gutan" paper... for... what we have.

                    PIP

     What do you have?

The two girls look around. One takes out something and
sets it on the counter. It is a BAGGIE OF POT, tied
with a pink ribbon.

Sarah and Pip look down, then at each other.

INT — PRINTSHOP PRODUCTION ROOM — NIGHT

Pip helps the two girls wheel a dolly outside with four
cases of bright orange flyers.

                  SARAH

     Later, tell your friends!

                 GIRL ONE

     Thank you, we will.

Sarah turns and walks into the back break room.

                  SARAH

     Yeah! We commerced the shit out of
     that order! Look at the time, it's
     4:20 already...

INT — MAGGIE'S KITCHEN — NIGHT

Maggie sits at her table drinking tea and reading a
book. Her wall clock reads 1:20. She sets her cup down.

                  MAGGIE

     "His hands don't have any scars."
     I notice things too. Who cares what
     he thinks?

She notices the book is upside down. She straightens it up, reads a line or two. Then drops it.

She rises, takes the cup to the sink and leaves the room. The light goes off.

INT — DAN'S BEDROOM — NIGHT

A clock on his desk reads 1:45 am. Dan sits at the table, reading mail, kinda zoned out. The logo for a publisher is across the top, first line reads "We regret that your work is not what we are looking for at this time."

> DAN
>
> Farmer. My ass.

He gets up and turns out the light.

EXT — 7-11 — DAY

Brad is talking on his cell across the street.

> BRAD
>
> I'm on my way right now. (pause) Yeah, total shit gig. I'll tell you more when you get to town. Later, bro.

He hangs up, then hurries across the parking lot and into Kopy King's back door.

INT — PRINTSHOP BREAK ROOM — DAY

Brad enters, he almost runs into Finny.

> BRAD
>
> Hey Finny.

> FINNY
>
> Who are you?

> BRAD
>
> Brad. I start today. Maggie hired me last Friday?

Finny sizes him up, makes a face

> FINNY
>
> Really? Huh. Go see Barry for your paperwork. Grab an apron from the rack, blah blah blah...

Finny hurries away not really caring if Brad heard him. Brad looks around and sees a rack holding yellow Kopy

King aprons. He goes to Maggie's office and opens the door.

                    BRAD

        Hey, Maggie, I need my paperwork and
        Barry isn't here...

Dan is behind the desk. He looks up.

                    DAN

        Most people knock before entering some-
        one's office. Or didn't you learn manners
        in Minnesota?

                    BRAD

        Oh. Beg your pardon. I was just...

                    DAN

        Late for work.

                    BRAD

        Uh, yeah. Sorry. I guess I'm just
        excited.

                    DAN

        Uh-huh. I think you'll find Barry at his
        desk.

                    BRAD

            Sure. Thanks.

Dan starts to walk out past him.

                    DAN

        Oh, I'm sorry, it was Oklahoma, wasn't
        it?

                    BRAD

        Huh? Oh, I mean, um...

                    DAN

        Thought so.

INT — PRINTSHOP PRODUCTION ROOM — DAY

Dan walks past Finny, who is on the phone, smiling.

                    FINNY

        I'm so sorry about that, ma'am. It was
        still wrong?

We hear loud French lady on other end. Finny smiles and
rolls his eyes.

                    FINNY

        I can not believe that. So I guess
        you'll have to come back in and tell me
        what you mean...

                    DAN

        You need help, Finny.

Finny covers the mouthpiece and whispers "She is SO
sexy," then uncovers the phone again.

Darla rushes in the front door from the street.

                    DARLA

        Sorry I'm late, Dan; I over slept.

                    DAN

        Long night again?

                    DARLA

        Ooh ...and crazy. There are some nasty
        people walking around out there.

                    DAN

        Then don't take their calls at all hours
        of the night "Mistress Tiniqua."

                    DARLA

        Need the money. Don't judge.

She rushes to the counter to clock-in then scurries to
the back. Barry walks up to him, flipping through some
papers.

                    BARRY

        One of these days she's gonna forget
        which job she's at.

                    DAN

        I want to be here when that happens.

Dan moves off toward Maggie, who works on the padding
machine and is finishing up as Dan reaches her.

                    DAN

        BoyToy's here.

Dan smirks and watches her apply padding compound with
a brush. She is making a mess.

                    MAGGIE

          He needs to get training.

                      DAN

          Yeah. Here.

Dan takes the brush from her and wipes the excess glue
from it. Then he wipes the glue off Maggie's arm with a
paper towel.

                      DAN

          I keep telling you, you don't need so
          much. A: you waste materials, and B: you
          make a mess of things.

                    MAGGIE

          I guess that's what happens when you lay
          it on too thick.

                      DAN

          I guess so.

They stare at each other a beat. Dan cracks first.

                      DAN

          Sorry. Had a rough day.

                    MAGGIE

          It's okay. Would you show him the
          counter, please, we really need to
          get him going.

                      DAN

          Has he got his Special Helmet on?

                    MAGGIE

          Knock it off, Dan.

She turns on the padder's heat blower, then heads up to
the counter to help customers.

Dan watches Brad, who is trying not to get close to
Barry as they go over paperwork. Barry tries to help
Brad tie his apron, but Brad keeps shifting away like
Barry has The Plague.

                    MIKE

          Morning Dan.

Dan looks around to Mike who is going over his work
list for the day.

> DAN
>
> Morning. Hey, think you can you keep
> your pants on next Thursday? Abe's
> coming in.

Mike sighs heavily.

> DAN
>
> This ain't Hippie Hollow, man. Deal
> with it.

Dan heads to Barry, who has Brad backed up against a
wall.

> DAN
>
> Quit playing with your food, Barry.

> BARRY
>
> Quit harshing my mellow, Dan.

Barry smiles at Brad and saunters away.

> DAN
>
> Ready to start on your new career, Brad?

> BRAD
>
> Please.

> DAN
>
> Let's go. We'll start with the counter,
> that's where you'll be primarily at
> first. It's what makes or breaks most
> orders. Poor counter service kills a
> company like Kopy King.

Brad chuckles a little.

> BRAD
>
> And leads to anarchy and the breakdown
> of civilization as we know it, right?

> DAN
>
> Fortunately, you weren't hired to be a
> world leader. You were hired to make
> copies. Make up your mind right now to
> do your best, or get the hell out.

The two stare at each other a second until Brad sees
Dan isn't kidding, then he smiles weakly.

> BRAD

Sorry, just kidding, Dan.

> DAN

(pause) This is what I do, so I take
some pride in it.

Dan walks away, pointing around the room. Brad rolls
his eyes and follows.

> DAN

Front counter — where orders come in and
go out. Production area... bindery and
finishing.

> BRAD

Right.

A nearby phone rings. Mike shouts to Brad.

> MIKE

Wanna get that, Brad?

Dan shoots a LOOK to Mike, smiles, then looks the OTHER
WAY OS. He pulls a laminated card out of his pocket and
hands it to Brad.

Brad looks for the phone under a bunch of papers and
answers it, reading from the card.

> BRAD

Thank you for calling Kopy King Down-
town, this is...

The shrill TONE of a fax machine is heard, Brad yanks
the phone from his ear.

> BRAD

Damn it.

> MIKE

What happened, man?

> BRAD

Apparently somebody got the fax and
phone numbers mixed up.

Brad hangs up, wiggling his pinky in his ear.

                    DAN

     That happens sometimes. They read the
     listing too fast.

The phone rings again.

                    MIKE

     There they go. Now they got it.

                    BRAD

     Thank you for calling Kopy King Down...

The high pitched TONE is heard again. Brad yanks the
phone away.

                    BRAD

     Motherfu...

Darla passes by tying her apron.

                    DARLA

     They do that to everybody first day.

Brad glances sideways at Dan, who looks OS screen
again, POV we see Finny at the fax machine; he and Dan
thumbs-up each other.

Darla makes a face at Dan, then goes to the counter
where MEGAN stands with her son TEDDY, 10-12 years old,
in a hockey jersey.

                    DARLA

     Hi Megan.

                    MEGAN

     Hi, Darla. We need to fax this order
     sheet, Teddy had his team pictures to-
     day. He's made first string!

                    DARLA

     Really? Congratulations, Teddy! You must
     be so proud, Megan!

                    MEGAN

     Thank you, I am!

Teddy is already off playing with things on the
counters; Dan motions for Brad to follow him.

                    DAN

     C'mon, Brad, Let's get it on. Mr. Finny!

                    FINNY

          Aye, Captain?

                     DAN

          A little training music please.

                    FINNY

          Yar!

Finny fiddles with the stereo just under the counter.
He settles on a station and we hear some cool alt-rock
start up.

                    FINNY

          Oh man! I love this song!

Montage of training scenes

A)   Barry shows Brad how to fill out a job ticket.

                    BARRY

          It's pretty self-explanatory, really.
          Name goes here. And if they want to
          wait on the job, use the green stick-
          ies and just put a "W" and leave it on
          the counter, here, and yell "black and
          white, or color, wait."

                    BRAD

          Do I ask them if they want fries with
          that?

                    BARRY

          Fries take about twenty minutes, we have
          to go next door for those.

Brad stares at Barry in disbelief.

                    BARRY

          It's a joke, sweetie.

B)   Brad works with Jerry then puts the job on the
counter. Jerry waves him back to make a change, then
sends him back to get a sticky note, then calls him
back to make other changes.

Brad gets confused and walks into the corner of the
counter. Jerry winces as Brad doubles over, holding
his groin.

C)   Darla shows Brad how to mount on foam core board.

                        DARLA

          Peel this backing off. Be careful, cause
          it's really sticky. If you put the pic-
          ture on wrong, it won't come back up.

Brad lightly touches the tacky surface, he has to pull
pretty hard to get his finger off.

                        BRAD

          Wow, that's pretty tacky.

                        DARLA

          Just like Friday night on Sixth Street,
          Baby.

D)   A FIDGETY MAN explains a complicated job to Brad
at warp speed. Brad just stares wide-eyed not knowing
what to do.

Finny intervenes and quickly takes the order. The man
leaves, but Brad doesn't move, Finny whacks him upside
the head.

E)   Dan and Maggie sit on a counter and watch as Mike
shows Brad how the folder works. Mike turns and bends
over to pick up a box of flyers.

Brad turns at the same moment and sees Mike's ASS. The
stack of folded papers in Brad's hands go flying.

Dan and Maggie roar.

F)   Brad tries to put down a poster on foam core, he
gets it wrong numerous times. The poster is getting
twisted and torn.

G)   Megan looks around the front of the store.

                        MEGAN

          Teddy? Where did you get to now?

H)   Dan is explaining counter etiquette to Brad with
Maggie and Darla looking on

                        DAN

          Don't judge what they bring in, or who
          they may seem like at first. They are
          just people, and they are the ones who
          pay our checks. Treat them all with the
          same respect and courtesy.

Someone catches Darla's eye. She points

                    DARLA

          GAAAAH! Church Lady!

Each scatters, pretending to be busy. Brad is left
at the counter as the CHURCH LADY — 50's, stern old
country — approaches.

                  CHURCH LADY

     Good morning. I have the glorious mis-
     sion to make copies of God's Word today.
     Would you help me?

                     BRAD

     Uh, sure, let's see what you have.

He starts to take a folder from her hand, but she stops
him with a strong grip on his wrist

                  CHURCH LADY

     Let us pray first, for the successful
     completion of this order, correctly, and
     on time.

She bows her head. Brad stares. She tightens her grip
and pulls Brad into the counter.

                  CHURCH LADY

     Bow, and pray with me. NOW.

Brad winces, and then bows.

I)   Brad has more trouble with the foam core. There
are pens and scissors, papers and a ruler stuck to the
board, as well as one of his hands. Teddy stands close
behind him.

                    TEDDY

     You're doing it wrong. You're doing it
     wrong. You're doing it wrong...

                     BRAD

     Shut up kid.

J)   Darla shows Brad how to hand place documents on
the copier. Brad's places one, then opens the lid too
soon and is blinded by the strobe. He staggers away and
knocks over stacks of papers, Finny holds a ream of
paper at crotch height and Brad rams his nuts again.

K)   Dan stands looking DOWN and shaking his head

                        DAN

        Jesus.

Dan's POV — Brad is lying on the floor stuck to the foam
core board along with numerous other objects... and
Teddy

                      TEDDY

        Owww... let me go... Mom!

End training montage

Finny finishes an air-guitar routine. Barry helps Brad
pick foam core out of his hair. Barry indicates Finny.

                      BARRY

        I would love to get that boy out for
        karaoke some night...

Darla holds a chunk of foam core with Teddy stuck to
it. She helps un-stick it.

                      DARLA

        Sorry about that... two minutes for
        boarding, right...?

Teddy growls at Brad, who winces as Barry pulls his
hair.

INT — MAGGIE'S OFFICE — DAY

Maggie watches from the other side of the two-way
mirror in her office and laughs. She checks out Brad's
butt as he walks around, then she sits at her desk.

                      MAGGIE

        Nice butt.

The door opens and Dan sticks his head in her office.

                        DAN

        Hey, by the way, I ordered all the
        paper and supplies. They'll be in late
        tomorrow.

                      MAGGIE

        Thanks. You're the best.

                        DAN

        Awwww... you noticed.

                      MAGGIE

        Hey, what's the count?

                    DAN

        Six. You want in?

Maggie pulls some money out of her pocket and throws
it.

                   MAGGIE

        Yeah. Eight.

                    DAN

        Nah. Gonna be an even dozen, easy.

He leaves. Maggie looks at MUG on her desk. It says
"Dick." On it.

DAYDREAM SEQUENCE

It is the Christmas party from the photo. Santa is
roaming and passing out gifts. He stops at Maggie and
Dan, who sit on a counter.

                   SANTA

        Have you both been good this year?

                   MAGGIE

        I haven't had time to be good, I work
        for a slave driver.

                    DAN

        Self-employed?

                   SANTA

        Oh, then I have a present for you, let's
        see what Santa has in his bag.

He digs through his bag and pulls out a wrapped box.

                   SANTA

        For Dan.

Dan opens the box. It is the Dick. Mug. Maggie frowns
at Santa.

                   MAGGIE

        Where's mine?

Santa fumbles in the bag

                   SANTA

        Santa thought bringing Dan to this store
        and making you the Area Manager would be
        enough this year. Here.

He pulls out a huge IOU sign from the bag and hands it to Maggie.

MAGGIE

Ahhh, That's much better.

Dan takes umbrage with a scoff.

DAN

I think this was supposed to be yours then.

SANTA

Don't feel so bad, Dan, she said you have a nice butt.

Maggie spits up her drink and her eyes grow wide. Dan and Santa laugh. Barry shouts over the party.

BARRY

Smile guys... newsletter.

They hug Santa and smile as the camera flashes.

END OF DAYDREAM

Maggie stands and stares through the mirror at Dan's butt as he walks away.

MAGGIE

Hmmmm.

INT — PRINTSHOP BREAK ROOM — DAY

Maggie, Dan, Brad and Barry are hanging up their aprons. Brad blows on his hands and fiddles with Band-Aids.

BARRY

A few paper cuts, Brad?

BRAD

Yeah. They hurt.

DAN

Looks like you got quite a few there. Like six or eight?

He glances quickly at Maggie, who sneers at him.

BRAD

I wish. More like a dozen. Ouch.

Dan grins back at Maggie. Brad leaves as Barry, Maggie and Dan watch.

Barry hands Dan a wad of money.

                    DAN

          And still undefeated. Thank you.

He fidgets a bit.

                    DAN

          Maggie, wanna go get something to eat?
          The Pho joint — is...

                    MAGGIE

          Uhhh, I... Can't.

                    DAN

          Sure, okay. No biggie

                    MAGGIE

          Sorry... I know you love that place...

He fidgets some more, looks away from Maggie, resumes swagger.

                    DAN

          Thanks for the money, suckers. Later.

He exits. Maggie stares after him.

                    MAGGIE

          How does he do that?

                    BARRY

          The winning? He's got friends.

Barry hangs up his apron and leaves.

                    MAGGIE

          What does that mean?

She shouts after Barry.

                    BARRY

          (sing-songy) He's got friends...

INT — PHO Joint — NIGHT

The place is pretty empty. Dan sits in a booth a cup of tea in front of him. He plays with his napkin.

He spots the COOK, KIM behind the counter, arguing

inaudibly with his WIFE. His gaze lingers before he looks back down to his napkin.

Dan looks up and sees a COUPLE at another table — cute, connected. The GUY imitates a monkey, Girl laughs.

                    DAN

          So easy a monkey can do it.

INT — PRINTSHOP PRODUCTION ROOM — DAY

Maggie looks at a stack of newly drilled paper. There are four holes, all at different spacings.

                    MAGGIE

          This is why not all the monkeys get
          bananas. Make sure the back guard is
          straight or the holes will all be dif-
          ferent widths from the edge. Also, um,
          they're 3-ring binders — not four.

                    BRAD

          Right.

She works at the press while Brad watches. Dan wanders by.

                    BRAD

          So, You and Dan work together a long
          time?

                    MAGGIE

          Yeah. He's been with us for about seven
          years. I've been here for maybe twelve,
          counting the years before Kopy King
          bought it.

                    BRAD

          Twelve years? Wow...

Maggie looks at him for a second.

                    MAGGIE

          It isn't exactly prison. I like it. Kopy
          King's is a decent company and I enjoy
          the people.

                    BRAD

          I'm sorry. I didn't mean...

                    MAGGIE

      I know. It's making copies. But I do en-
      joy it. You meet interesting people, and
      help solve their problems.

                     BRAD

      So, Dan like his work, too?

Maggie spies Dan walking toward Finny.

                    FINNY

      Dan, Muscle Car calendars... does the
      color look right to you...

Dan walks up and looks at the job in Finny's hands — a
pin-up calendar for a mechanic's shop.

                    MAGGIE

      He's something, huh? I don't know why he
      stays.

Dan "examines" the job more closely.

                     DAN

      Hmm, may have to run some more, drop the
      cyan, add some pink.

                    MAGGIE

      He's a writer. I guess he stays for the
      free copies.

                     BRAD

      Writer, huh? Poet, I'll bet. Dark and
      brooding?

Dan and Finny flip through the calendar, grinning
widely.

                    FINNY

      Was it that cold in March?

Dan and Finny laugh. Dan looks up and his gaze meets
Maggie's.

Her eyes narrow into slits. The smile fades from Dan's
face. He slaps Finny on the back of the head.

                     DAN

      Come on, Finny, box it up, you're not
      supposed to be looking through people's
      orders. (whispering) Save me one.

Finny nods. Dan walks away looking for something to do.
Maggie smirks and gets back to Brad.

> MAGGIE
>
> No. At least not often. He likes to hit
> the coffee bars and make fun of the col-
> lege kids with goatees who would like to
> be dark and brooding.

She pulls the stack of paper out of the drill press and
shows Brad the three neat holes.

> MAGGIE
>
> See? Even. Don't let the drill sit in
> the paper too long or it'll burn. Think
> you can do the rest?

> BRAD
>
> Yeah, sure.

> MAGGIE
>
> Good. Finish this up, then clean up by
> noon. The owner is coming in today for a
> meeting.

Maggie walks away. Brad sizes up the job and mutters
under his breath.

> BRAD
>
> This ought to be good. Pimple-faced copy
> nerd boy.

He starts to drill, the press hits his thumb.

> BRAD
>
> God damn it.

Brad sticks his thumb in his mouth. Mike looks up from
his folding, sniggers and shakes his head.

> MIKE
>
> Dick.

INT — PRINTSHOP PRODUCTION ROOM — DAY

Brad puts a piece of paper on the order counter.

> BRAD
>
> Black and white wait.

MRS. WOLFENHABER — 70's, your favorite grandma, had a

rough life — enters the store. She smiles at Brad, and
he meets her at the counter.

                    BRAD

          Hi, what can I do for you?

                MRS. WOLFENHABER

          Hello, young man. Is Dan here?

                    BRAD

          No ma'am. My name's Brad, I can help
          you.

                MRS. WOLFENHABER

          Oh. I normally work with Dan. I need
          copies of some pictures. I have them
          here.

She starts to get a packet out of her bag, but her
hands don't work so well. Brad gets bored waiting and
drags the packet out for her.

                    BRAD

          There. If you need help, just ask.

                MRS. WOLFENHABER

          Thank you. I can do it myself, these
          pictures are very delicate, very old.

She takes them out one by one. Brad looks down at them
and laughs.

                    BRAD

          Man, that is one funny looking kid. When
          were these taken, a thousand years ago?

                MRS. WOLFENHABER

          That was my sister. She's dead.
          Consumption.

Darla comes up next to Brad.

                    DARLA

          Good afternoon, Mrs. Wolfenhaber, how
          are you today?

                MRS. WOLFENHABER

          Oh, Hi, Darla, I was wondering if Dan
          could help me with my book.

                    DARLA

     Oh, I think he's here by now, Mrs.
     Wolfenhaber. Let me go get him. Uh,
     Brad, let me show you where the break
     room is.

She turns toward the woman.

                    DARLA

     He's new.

                    WOMAN

     I'll take the older model, please.

She chuckles and Darla smiles as she leads Brad off.

                    BRAD

     What's her problem?

                    DARLA

     She just needs a little extra attention.
     She's a regular. Comes in every week on
     the bus. You'll know who's who soon.

                    BRAD

     Yeah, I guess so.

                    DARLA

     Hey, Brad, you taking lunch? Wanna go
     hit Sidelines — it's a sports bar just
     down the street?

                    BRAD

     Sounds great, but not today, Darla. I,
     uh, have to meet my sister for lunch.

                    DARLA

     No problem. Catch you on the flip side,
     huh?

She winks at him.

INT — PRINTSHOP HALLWAY — DAY

                    BRAD

     Sure. No problem.

Darla goes into the office and Dan comes out shortly
thereafter. He walks out to help Mrs. Wolfenhaber.

                    BRAD

      (under his breath) Weenie.

He turns and checks out the employee bulletin board on
the wall. There are notices about meetings, safety,
monthly projections.

Marked in red is a pool for how long it'll take 'til
"Brad gets fired". Dan put fifty dollars on Nov. 18.

                    BRAD

      Up yours.

ABE SPINETTI — 70ish, easy-going, the embodiment of
"been-there-done-that, what's next?" — comes around the
corner and looks about the hallway. He is dressed in
nice-ish clothes, but they are wrinkled.

                    ABE

      Hello?

                    BRAD

      Excuse me. Are you lost?

                    ABE

      What?

                    BRAD

      Do you need some help? The counter is
      that way.

He gestures.

                    ABE

      No, I was looking...

                    BRAD

      Like I said, if you can follow me, I'll
      show you to the counter.

                    ABE

      Who are you, young man?

                    BRAD

      I'm Brad. I work here. You are?

Maggie walks from behind Brad.

                    MAGGIE

      Mr. Spinetti, how are you?

                         MAN

          I'm fine, Maggie, and for the last time,
          call me Abe. I hate that "Mr. Spinetti,"
          and "Sir" shit.

Maggie comes forward and shakes the Abe's hand.

                       MAGGIE

          Mr... Abe, this is Brad Mann, our
          new counter person. Brad, this is Abe
          Spinetti, Kopy King's owner.

                        BRAD

          Sorry, Abe, I...

                        ABE

          You can call me Mr. Spinetti.

The three just kind of stare at each other a beat.

                        ABE

          I heard the counter is that way.

He points, Brad retreats. Abe watches him go then looks
at Maggie with an impish grin.

                       MAGGIE

          What, you too? Jesus, we needed a new
          counter person.

Abe snickers and walks into Maggie's office, as she
heads the other way.

                       MAGGIE

          Let me get Dan.

She passes by Mike who is wearing a SPEEDO.

                       MAGGIE

          Thanks for the effort, Mike.

Mike nods and makes his way into the breakroom.

INT — MAGGIE'S OFFICE — DAY

Maggie, Barry, Dan and Abe sit around the desk. Abe
leans back in his chair, looking around the table.

                        ABE

          Okay, anyway, enough small talk. Here's
          the deal. I know you all have been real-
          ly busy lately, and I hate to pile any-

thing else on your plates, but Kopy King
is undergoing what we in the business
call a re-ordering.

A collective groan goes up from the table.

                    ABE

Now listen to me. It's not exactly what
you think. No one is going to lose their
jobs, except for that ass clown Jimmy
over at the UT store. It probably won't
affect your day to day routine much.
But times change, and it is time for a
change... change is... coming...

                    DAN

What are you trying not to say, Abe.

                    ABE

Can't really discuss in detail right
now. But when the dust settles, there
will be some bonuses for the long term
people, and more profit sharing for all
employees...

                    MAGGIE

But?

                    BARRY

Here it comes.

Abe shifts uneasily in his chair.

                    ABE

But, until then we can't afford any new
equipment, or overtime. Or new hires.
And that extension into the space next
door will have to wait.

                    MAGGIE

What?! We are all working extra hours as
it is and we're barely getting everything done. No overtime!?

                    DAN

Crying out loud, Abe. We're still using
a 9500. A 9500! That's what Moses used
to make copies of the Ten Commandments.

                         BARRY

This is wedding season. I'm working ten
hours a day and I'm still behind.

                         MAGGIE

Oh boo hoo. Every month is wedding
season to you, Barry.

                         BARRY

Hey, I bring in almost twenty percent of
the monthly nut, girlfriend.

                         MAGGIE

You're a monthly nut.

                          DAN

Fight, fight. Kick his ass, Maggie.

                         BARRY

Really, Dan? REALLY?

                          ABE

Come on, guys. I'm not Kopy King anymore. It's out of my hands. After next
month... I won't even be a share holder.

                         MAGGIE

What? Abe...

                          ABE

Look, I started as a printer's appren-
tice when I was fifteen. By the time I
was eighteen, I was doing business on
the side, using my boss' equipment. I
pulled in each month nearly as much as
the shop did in a week. One day the
owner caught me, and said I had moxie.
"Kid, you've got moxie," he said, "some
day you're gonna be the Copy King!" and
the name stuck. You know, I've always
hated that name. Copies have literal-
ly been my life since then. (pause) I'm
tired of copies, Maggie. It's an iffy in-
dustry at best in this digital age, and
they want to push me out to make room
for this "young blood" that everybody
keeps talking about. Besides... I just

need to do something... new. So... I'm
leaving.

There is a moment or two of silence. Everyone stares at
the wall or their feet.

                    ABE

It had to happen some day. Business
isn't like it was when I started. I
don't like it, I don't like the way
these new folks work, and I can't keep
up the pace. I like you guys cause
you're family, but,

                    DAN

You like us cause we're the number one
store in Austin. Where are you going?

                    ABE

I'll be consulting and working on my tan
for a year or so, but after that

Abe shrugs. Barry is almost in tears.

                    BARRY

I can't... stand it. I'm sorry.

He excuses himself and gets up and leaves the room.

                    ABE

What's with Barry. He on his period?

                    MAGGIE

Oh Abe, this the worst... news...

                    ABE

It's not like I'm dying, call me whenever you want. Anybody want to go get a
calzone from Pizzo's? Better yet, you
two go grab a bite and commiserate —
I'll buy us a steak tomorrow, okay? Go
on, I'm going to the hotel.

INT — MR. FISH AND CHIPS SHOP — DAY

Dan and Maggie order fish and chips at the counter. They
take their drinks and go get a seat.

                    DAN

Maggie, it's not the end of the world.

                    MAGGIE

        It might as well be. Abe's selling out.

                      DAN

        He's being muscled out. That's how busi-
        ness gets done now.

Maggie gives him a look as they sit down.

                      DAN

        Look, A: You were the same way when Kopy
        King bought Congress Copies, remember?
        And B: It'll still be Kopy King, just
        owned by someone else.

                    MAGGIE

        No, Dan. They're going to "merge"
        like businesses do now. Then everything
        goes to crap. The sense of family will
        disappear.

                      DAN

        Congress Copies.

                    MAGGIE

        No. Congress Copies was running in the
        red, they were ready to close, and the
        owner was a jive-ass jerk.

                      DAN

        Heh-heh... you said "Jive-ass." (gig-
        gles) Yeah, but the NEW owner wasn't.

The cook KIM brings out their order.

                      KIM

        I give you free fry zucchini. Sorry took
        so long.

                      DAN

        Hey, thanks, Kim.

Kim nods and returns to the kitchen.

                      DAN

        Take a look at Kim. He and his wife took
        over this dump of a store a couple years
        ago, and now it's the best food in the
        area.

We hear shouting in Korean from the kitchen, Kim and
his WIFE, accompanied by banging pots and pans.

Maggie, Dan and a few other patrons don't even react to
it. Others in the store are taken aback.

                         MAGGIE

          And you get a free floor show.

                         DAN

          And yet people still pack this joint —
          every day. Change can be good.

The yelling gets louder. The kitchen door swings open
and a smiling Kim returns with someone's order.

                         MAGGIE

          You think they've been like that all
          their lives?

                         DAN

          Not yet. But they probably will be.

                         MAGGIE

          How can they stand it?

                         DAN

          Everybody has their moments, I guess.
          You just try to make sure one outweighs
          the other.

They stare at each other for a beat. They eat as Kim
returns to the kitchen and the arguing continues.

                         DAN

          Probably just mad at her cause she works
          too much and never has time for him.

                         MAGGIE

          Or maybe he never communicates except
          through a complicated series of grunts
          and snarls that frighten people.

                         DAN

          Nah. It's her.

                         MAGGIE

          You think so?

                         DAN

          Yeah, I think so.

                       MAGGIE

          Who cares what you think.

Dan shrugs, eats his food.

INT — PRINTSHOP BREAK ROOM — DAY

Darla fixes a cup of coffee, she looks tired. Finny waits
his turn. Barry puts his apron on.

                       BARRY

               TGIF kids.

                       DARLA

               No shit, baby. This week was a bear. I'm
               exhausted.

                       FINNY

               What do you do while you're on the phone
               all night that gets you so tired, Darla.

                       BARRY

               No freebies, Finny. Get your credit card
               out and call her.

                       FINNY

          Damnit.

Brad exits Maggie's office. Maggie is holding a small
bunch of flowers.

                       MAGGIE

               Thank you so much, Brad, they're beauti-
               ful.

                       BRAD

               I see them on the side of the road every
               day, I thought you might want some to
               brighten up your office, so I picked 'em.

Darla shoots a glance to Finny and whispers.

                       DARLA

          Don't they sell those...

                       FINNY

          (Nods)...at the Stop-N-Rob.

                    MAGGIE

    I never get fresh flowers. Thank you.

                     BRAD

    No problem. You deserve them.

Brad goes to the production room. Barry, Finny and
Darla just stare. Maggie looks up at the them.

                    MAGGIE

        What?

Barry shakes his head and leaves.

                    BARRY

        One-trick-pony-assed farm boy.

                    MAGGIE

        What?

                    FINNY

        I'm gonna go see if DAN needs anything.

He leaves. Darla glares at Maggie and leaves.

                    MAGGIE

        What? What?

INT — PRINTSHOP PRODUCTION ROOM — DAY

Barry brings an order to Dan at the delivery table.

                    BARRY

        Here's the engagement notices for the
        Hurley's, Dan. Needs to go out today.

                     DAN

        Thanks, Barry.

Barry stands and stares at Dan, who doesn't notice for
a moment, then finally turns.

                     DAN

        What, man?

                    BARRY

        Okay. Well, I gotta go order the Jeffer-
        son Wedding cards...

                     DAN

        They're already in.

                    BARRY

     You sure?

                    DAN

     Yeah, in Maggie's office, I'll go get 'em
     for you.

                    BARRY

     Oooh... Thanks.

Dan sets down the work he has and leaves. Barry smiles
and goes back to his desk.

INT — MAGGIE'S OFFICE — DAY

Dan enters Maggie's office and looks around.

                    DAN

          Here, Jefferson Wedding shit, here boy.

He starts to whistle as if for a dog. He spies the
flowers on her desk. He reads the note.

                    DAN

          "Maggie, so glad I met you — Thanks for
          everything, Brad."

INT — PRINTSHOP PRODUCTION ROOM — DAY

Maggie walks up to Dan, who is busy at the cutter. She
can only see Dan's head and shoulders behind it.

                    MAGGIE

     Dan, got a minute?

                    DAN

     Sure, just let me finish this up first.

                    MAGGIE

     No, you can keep working. I just need
     you to check in on second shift again.
     I'm getting customers calling in.

Dan makes a few more cuts, adjusting it each time.

                    DAN

     They're alright.

                    MAGGIE

     So you don't mind checking in on them
     tonight?

Dan looks down at his work with a heavy sigh.

                    MAGGIE

     You can? Is that a yes or no? (pause)
     Why don't you go in before we meet Abe
     tonight, OK?

                     DAN

     Uh huh.

                    MAGGIE

     Thanks. Need any help with that?

                     DAN

     Nope.

She waits for more, then throws up her hands and
leaves.

                    MAGGIE

     What is it with you men and the
     grunting?

Dan finishes, then scoops pieces of Maggie's flowers into
a box and throws it on the QC table.

                     DAN

     Quality Check.

INT — PRINTSHOP PRODUCTION ROOM — NIGHT

Dan enters. Cici and Stephanie are at the counter
talking with Jerry who has four boxes of books. Dan
watches from behind.

                    JERRY

     When I called a few hours ago, you said
     I could get these bounded while I wait.

                   STEPHANIE

     Sir, you said you had a dozen or so
     books half an inch thick. You've got
     a hundred fifty books here. And they're
     thicker.

                    JERRY

     You said you could bindicate thirty
     books in fifteen minutes, so this should
     only take you about an hour. I've got a
     class to teach tomorrow morning.

                          CICI

          It's not that easy, Jerry, and that was
          a few hours ago.

                          JERRY

          Mister Speedy Print — could do it.

Stephanie and Dan make eye contact. Dan comes up to the
counter.

                          DAN

          They let you out at night now, Jerry?

                          JERRY

          I asked these ladies on the phone if
          they could...

                          DAN

          I heard that. Look, taking a few minutes
          to bind a couple books is one thing, but
          taking all of our time to bind five times
          as many takes eight times as long. We
          can do it by ten pm, we only have two
          people on this shift, and they're busy.

Stephanie raises an eyebrow, "told you so." Jerry gets
persnickety.

                          JERRY

          Well, then maybe I'll take it to Mister
          Speedy Print

                          DAN

          Go right ahead and take it to Mister
          Speedy print, Jerry. They ain't open
          all night.

                          JERRY

          Fine, I'll go in the morning.

                          DAN

          Good. Maybe they'll have it done by
          four, I'll bet your class is way before
          that.

                          JERRY

          I mean it, I'll take my business to
          Mister Speedy Print

                    DAN

          Fine, Jerry, go to Mister Speedy Print

Jerry glares at Dan, but is no match, he starts to
weaken.

                    DAN

          What are you waiting for? Mister Speedy
          Print — opens at eight, ask for Ron,
          he's usually sober by noon.

Jerry looks at his shoes.

                    DAN

          You're not going, are you?

                    JERRY

          No.

                    DAN

          And why is that?

Jerry mumbles.

                    DAN

          What was that?

                    JERRY

          Cause Mister Speedy Print — sucks.

                    DAN

          Because Mister Speedy Print — sucks.

                    JERRY

          Ok, I'll leave it, and pick it up at
          ten pm.

                    DAN

          Sorry, we took in three new jobs since
          you called. Come back at twelve. It'll
          be done. Right ladies?

                    CICI

          Yeah, Dan, no problem.

                    DAN

          Thank you Jerry, have a great evening.

                    JERRY

          DOCTOR...

Dan rolls his eyes and snorts as Jerry slinks away. Dan turns to Cici and Stephanie.

                    DAN

     So what's going on?

                    STEPHANIE

     Huh?

                    DAN

     I heard you guys aren't getting jobs
     done on time etc etc.

                    CICI

     Same as first shift — too much work. Don
     is useless.

                    DAN

     We fired Don. (off quizzical looks) You
     didn't notice he wasn't here?

                    STEPHANIE

     Ahh. That's why Maggie said that you
     were going to help us out for a few
     days.

                    DAN

     She what now?

                    STEPHANIE

     Yeah.

                    CICI

     She said you said you didn't mind.

                    DAN

     Why would I mind? A: I've got no life,
     and B: who needs to work on some stupid
     novel anyway?

Cici and Stephanie watch him mutter and stalk away.

                    DAN

     At least I get to have dinner with Abe
     tonight. He's fun to be around.

INT — STEAK HOUSE — NIGHT

Abe, Maggie and Dan sit at a table. Dan and Maggie pick at a plate of onion rings on the table.

166

                    ABE

     Jesus, when did Austin get so hipstery,
     crowded and expensive?

                    DAN

     It's been a few years, Abe. Things
     change fast here now.

Abe looks at the menu.

                    ABE

     These freakin steaks cost more than a
     whole damn cow.

                    DAN

     Steer. Cows give milk.

                    ABE

     Well, they sure as hell are milking
     these prices. We didn't go into Ruth's
     Cris because it was too expensive just
     to read the sign. I thought this place
     was still cheap.

                    DAN

     You mean inexpensive.

                    MAGGIE

     Are we going to talk about prices all
     night?

                    DAN

     Yeah, maybe we should all get back to
     work and work on some more work.

Dan and Maggie exchange a look as the waiter
approaches.

                    WAITRESS

     Have we decided yet?

                    ABE

     Yes. But we'll eat here anyway. Do you
     have any steaks that cost less than my
     dialysis?

Maggie grabs the menu out of his hands.

                    MAGGIE

     Good lord. He'll have the prime rib.

                              DAN

          Did you ask? Maybe he doesn't want the
          prime rib.

                            MAGGIE

          Maybe I don't care.

                              DAN

          I think we should ask him.

                            MAGGIE

          Who cares what you think?

                              DAN

          God forbid it was you.

The waitress and Abe look back and forth at the two.
Abe tries to interrupt a few times and gives up.

                            MAGGIE

          What the hell is that supposed to mean?

                              DAN

          I think you know what I'm talking about.

                            MAGGIE

          Do I? You never say enough for me to get
          a trace on it.

                              DAN

          Well, then why don't you just make up
          what you want me to say. You're the only
          one you ever pay attention too anyway.

                            MAGGIE

          I pay attention to everyone.

                              DAN

          If by "everyone" you mean Brad, I agree.

Maggie throws down her napkin and storms off. Abe looks
up at the Waitress.

                              ABE

          I'll have the Prime Rib. And a pitcher
          of tequila.

                            WAITRESS

          (Indicating Dan) And you sir?

Dan just glares up at her

MAGGIE — no, WAITRESS

WAITRESS

O-kay. I'll be back in a minute.

She scurries off. Dan mouths the word "Shit"

INT — LADY'S ROOM DOORWAY — NIGHT

Maggie exits. She sees Dan and Abe talking across the room. She looks away and does a double take.

MAGGIE

What the...

She sees Brad getting up from a table at the other end of the room. She follows him as he heads for the door. Just before he leaves she stops him.

MAGGIE

I must be paying you too much.

Brad is startled and turns to see her.

BRAD

What? Oh... uh... hi... Maggie.

MAGGIE

I must be paying you too much if you can afford to eat here.

BRAD

Ooh. I'm caught. Actually, I, uh, I was applying for a job here.

MAGGIE

Wha...what? Are you leaving...

BRAD

Oh, no, no. But my sister just got laid off, so I'm taking a second job to help her out with rent. Since I live with her. And her kids.

MAGGIE

Oh, I'm sorry, Brad. I just...

Brad gets a gleam in his eye.

BRAD

You want to go for a walk, Maggie? Maybe get a cup of coffee?

                              MAGGIE

          Well, I kind of...

Maggie glances back to where Dan and Abe are. Dan is
gesticulating about like a mad Monk.

                              MAGGIE

          You know what? Yes.

                              BRAD

          Great! I kind of wanted to see some more
          of downtown, the lights make me feel
          like a kid again. Not that there was
          anything that fancy back in, uh... Okla-
          homa.

They head out the door.

INT — STEAK HOUSE — NIGHT

Dan is ending his tirade. Abe is visibly bored, eating
breadsticks.

                              DAN

          That's all I'm saying. Am I right, or am
          I wrong?

Abe doesn't answer

                              DAN

          Well?

Abe comes out of his faux stupor.

                              ABE

          Huh? Oh, my turn now?

Dan grabs a breadstick and takes a huge chomp.

                              ABE

          Dan, I've known you for seven years. For
          three of those you have been trying to
          get Maggie to notice you.

                              DAN

          What?

                              ABE

          Oh, for Christ's sake, kid, give me some
          credit.

Dan concedes and goes back to eating his bread stick.

                    ABE

     But your problem is you're a good writ-
     er, not a good talker. You hate being
     wrong, and so you never are — yes that
     was facetious — and you can not for the
     life of you express yourself to the one
     you love.

                    DAN

     (grumbling) Love is a pretty strong
     word.

                    ABE

     Yes. It is. Makes you act like a dick-
     head sometimes.

Dan looks up at Abe with a silent question.

                    ABE

     (nods) Yes. You are. (pause) So, how is
     that novel coming along?

The waitress arrives with the food and sets it on the
table.

                    DAN

     It's still out to Prometheus Publishing.
     They're the only ones I haven't heard
     back from yet.

                    ABE

     Prometheus? They're good. No news is
     good news, I'm sure. Keep the faith.

Dan grunts. The waitress puts a plate in front of Abe.

                    WAITRESS

     Prime rib.

                    ABE

     Thank you.

The waitress flinches as she puts the plate in front of
Dan and hurries out of his way. Dan looks up.

                    DAN

      Sorry.

                    WAITRESS

     Enjoy your meals.

                    ABE

          Come on, eat, we'll talk, Maggie will
          walk around and cool her ass off, you'll
          see her tomorrow. Okay? Okay.

They dig into their meals.

EXT — CONGRESS AVE. — NIGHT

Maggie and Brad walk toward the bridge. Brad looks up
at the lights and finishes a hamburger. Maggie drinks
from a supersize cup.

                    BRAD

          So... copies. You ever want to do some-
          thing else? Something bigger?

                    MAGGIE

          Like what? Change the world? Save peo-
          ple? No, not really. I'll leave that
          to the people who do that well. I'm not
          much of a people person.

                    BRAD

          I think you sell yourself short. I've
          seen you at work, everyone likes you.

                    MAGGIE

          (snorting) Yeah, well, not everybody.

                    BRAD

          Well... I like you.

Maggie stops, then Brad stops and turns to her. She
leans in toward him, but he suddenly pulls away as
something catches his attention.

                    BRAD

          Cool! Is that the Bat Bridge?!

He heads down the street; Maggie rolls her eyes and
follows.

                    MAGGIE

          What is it with men and those damn bats?

INT — MAGGIE'S OFFICE — NIGHT

Dan sits at Maggie's desk and picks up the phone and
dials.

                    DAN

         Come on, come on

Voicemail picks up.

                    MAGGIE'S VO

         Hello, this is Maggie, leave a message
         and I'll get back to you.

                    DAN

         Hey, Mag, It's me, Dan. I just called to
         apol... to say I'm...

He stops and thinks.

                    DAN

         I'm sorry I was a dickhead tonight. I'll
         see you Monday. (beat) Oh, no I won't.
         I forgot, I've got to open the UT store
         for Jimmy, and then work my second shift
         here. See you when I see you.

He hangs up and stares at the wall.

INT — PRINTSHOP PRODUCTION ROOM — NIGHT

Sarah and Pip lean on the counter reading documents as
Dan drags his ass from the office.

                    SARAH

         Taking off man?

                    DAN

         Yep. You guys have a good night.

                    PIP

         Hey, Dan, check this out, man.

Dan lumbers over to the counter, sees what they are
reading.

                    DAN

         Oh, for crying out loud, guys, these are
         court documents.

                    SARAH

         Yeah, pretty dry reading, but look here.
         These are transcripts from the Porter
         brothers' trial.

                    DAN

          God damn it, guys, put that shit away.

                    PIP

          Look who they mention here...

                    DAN

          Wortner and Girten, Accountants.

                    PIP

          We just finished their job. They had all
          this shit listed in their files, expenses
          and stuff. There's all these huge pay-
          ments made to the Stetson Club marked
          "bonuses and incentives."

                    DAN

          And?

                    SARAH

          What kind of accountants pay a music
          venue? And look at the amounts. They're
          laundering money, man.

Dan looks at the records again, then up at Sarah and
Pip. He shakes his head.

                    DAN

          Lay off the wine coolers and Yo-ho's,
          guys. You shouldn't be reading these.
          You don't know anything about this.

                    PIP

          What? Organized Crime?

                    DAN

They were acquitted in court, remember?

                    SARAH

          Oh, yeah, that defamation suit, the one
          where their character witnesses from New
          York, Jimmy "the Weasel" Graffoni and
          Bobby "the Chin" Falcone, said they
          never heard of any gangland ties.

                    DAN

          Yeah. Good. Call the FBI. Do your damn
          jobs and leave that shit alone.

Dan heads out as Pip and Sarah read documents while
working.

                         PIP

          Later, man.

Dan leaves as BETTY FUDDER enters. She is dressed like
a hooker. She plops a box filled with assorted colored
papers on the counter.

                        BETTY

          Excuse me. How much are copies if I do
          them on my own paper?

Sarah looks in the box. The papers are wrinkled and
have stains and staple holes.

                        SARAH

          Four cents each, ma'am. Hey, aren't you
          Wanda Touchem? You used to dance at Mus-
          tang Mary's.

The woman pulls one page out of the box, Pip comes over
to see. The hand-written flyer has a picture of Betty on
it.

                        BETTY

          That's right! My real name is Betty
          Fudder, I'm running for mayor. Could
          you run my flyer on this paper. There's
          about, I don't know... a bunch here.

Pip looks at the boxed paper. Her opponents' flyers are
printed on the backs.

                         PIP

          We just printed these yesterday.

                        SARAH

          Is that ethical, ma'am?

                        BETTY

          What? Recycling?

                        SARAH

          You pulled them all down.

                         PIP

          (shrugs) None of our business. Okay,
          it'll be a few minutes.

Pip takes the box and starts to pull out stacks and re-jog them into neat piles.

INT — PRINTSHOP PRODUCTION ROOM — DAY

Mike works at the folder. Darla makes blueprint — copies for a man. Finny is on the phone.

A man, HECTOR, walks up to the counter and Brad greets her.

> BRAD
>
> Hi, what can I do for you?

> HECTOR
>
> I'm here to pick up an order for Hinojosa. Business plans. Photos.

> BRAD
>
> Ok, hang on.

Brad goes over to the completed job cubbies and finds the box. He places it on the counter,

> BRAD
>
> There you are, you may want to check it over.

Brad rings up the order as Hector looks through it. Finny watches blankly as he talks on the phone at the end of the counter.

> HECTOR
>
> This looks great. You guys really did a good job with the photos. You ran this?

Brad sees DAN's NAME in the "completed by" box on the ticket. He crumples it up, looks around and sees nobody watching.

> BRAD
>
> Yeah, yes I did.

Hector gives Brad a visa, then drops a twenty on the counter.

> HECTOR
>
> That's for you. Thank you SO much, man.

Brad stuffs the money in his pocket. Finny stops talking and uncrumples the ticket... sees Dan's name... stares at Brad.

As Brad turns to leave, Finny re-adjusts himself so
that Brad can't see that he saw what happened.

Maggie comes out of her office and heads straight for
Finny with a piece of paper in her hand.

> MAGGIE

Finny, did you help a Ms. Duquesne earlier this month? And then again when she
came in to pick up?

> FINNY

Oh, let me see, um... name sounds
familiar.

> MAGGIE

Well she just called. She seems to be
having problems with her job, which is
back on the QC table yet again. She's
not happy at all.

> FINNY

Is she really pissed?

He looks positively giddy. Maggie looks askance at him.

> MAGGIE

Yes. She is. Take care of it, would you
please? You sick little troll.

> FINNY

Sure. Okay. Yes. Yes. Yes.

She hands him the paper and walks off. Finny clutches
the paper and does a tiny victory dance

Brad flips through brochures on the QC table and
overhears the exchange. He looks around the table and
sees a box marked "Duquesne."

Maggie walks over to him and pats him on the shoulder.

> MAGGIE

Brad, you can leave whenever you want,
we're pretty slow today.

> BRAD

No problem. Hey, uh, you free tonight?

> MAGGIE

What? Yeah, I guess. I can. Be. Why.

                    BRAD

Oh, I don't mean to be too forward, but
my sister is letting me have a night off
from watching her kids. So I thought I'd
go see a movie or music or something.

                  MAGGIE

Um. okay. I'm taking Abe to the airport,
but after that I'm free.

                    BRAD

Which?

                  MAGGIE

Huh?

                    BRAD

Movie or music?

                  MAGGIE

Uh... I... oh gosh..

                    BRAD

Maybe Barry's show?

                  MAGGIE

I've seen it... And he should stick to
wedding invitations.

                    BRAD

Bad?

                  MAGGIE

Just not into guys who can't sing
dressed as women who can't sing. Anyway, I'm sure we can find something to do
together that doesn't involve clothes. I
mean women's clothes. I won't be wearing
them — I mean I normally wear...

                    BRAD

Either way.

Maggie slinks away, a little embarrassed.

Brad smiles and goes back to his work. Mike is watching
in the background. He isn't happy at all.

EXT — AIRPORT PARKING — DAY

Maggie and Abe sit in a car in the parking garage.

                    ABE

     Who was that charming woman I met at the
     counter today?

                    MAGGIE

     Mrs. Wolfenhaber? She's a regular.

                    ABE

     I liked her. Nice. Smart woman. She said
     she's working on a book?

                    MAGGIE

     Yeah, a photo book. She's been working
     on it for three years. It's about her
     family. Really sad. Illness and acci-
     dents. Now she has nobody.

                    ABE

     It sucks not to have anybody.

                    MAGGIE

     How come you never married, Abe?

                    ABE

     Aw, I cared too much about my business.
     Now look at me, I'm rich. But I can't
     have sex with my money.

                    MAGGIE

     There are places you can in this town.

Abe makes a face.

                    ABE

     Yuck. I'd need to shower for a week.
     What about you, Maggie, anybody in your
     life?

                    MAGGIE

     No. Not really. I don't... know.

Abe thinks they are on the same page.

                    ABE

     Stop wasting time, Maggie. Before you
     know it you're old and lonely like me
     and Mrs. Wolf Blitzer.

                    MAGGIE

     Wolfenhaber.

                     ABE

     Whatever. You have to save time for
     yourself... and make room for that spe-
     cial someone else. It shouldn't be that
     hard — take a good look at the person
     you're with. How do they make you feel?
     Do you think about them when they aren't
     around? Don't be a dickhead, and you'll
     do fine in any relationship. Go for it.
     Now let me out, I'll miss my plane.

                    MAGGIE

     It leaves in two hours.

                     ABE

     TSA wants to poke around my colostomy
     bag for an hour. I've been eating pop-
     corn and prunes all night just for them.

Maggie opens her door and goes around the back of the
car to get Abe's bags out. Abe gets out to help.

                    MAGGIE

     Come back soon, Abe.

                     ABE

     I'll be back. Don't work so hard.

                    MAGGIE

     I won't.

They hug and Abe kisses her on the forehead. Then he
takes his bags and goes into the airport.

INT — PRINTSHOP PRODUCTION ROOM — DAY

Barry and Dan stand at the counter, it is slow. Darla
leans on the end of the counter trying to stay awake
while filling out a form.

                    BARRY

     It's happening.

The phone rings, Barry answers.

                    BARRY

     Thank you for calling Kopy King Down-
     town. (Pause) Hold please.

He hits the intercom button, his voice is heard
throughout the store.

> BARRY
>
> Production. Line two. Mistress
> Tiniqua, line two.

Darla wearily reaches for the phone next to her and
answers in a soft, sexy voice.

> DARLA
>
> Hey baby, who is this? Hi, Steve, what
> do you want to talk about tonight? Ooh,
> you want me to what? You want me to do
> that with my clothes on or off, baby.

She goes on in her sexy phone voice. Barry and Dan are
dying. Finny walks over.

> FINNY
>
> Aw, tell her already.

> BARRY
>
> Hang on. I want to hear what he does.

> DARLA
>
> Ooh, you nasty boy, you into bondage?
> What? Binding? You want to what?

She suddenly becomes wide awake and is flustered.

> DARLA
>
> I'm, I'm sorry, you have the, the wrong
> number.

She slams down the phone and looks at Dan and Barry.

> DARLA
>
> Who was that?

> BARRY
>
> Customer. Needed some books bound.

> DARLA
>
> Oh my God. Dan.

> DAN
>
> You naughty, dirty girl.

Darla covers her mouth and runs back toward the break
room. Finny stares after her.

INT — PRINTSHOP BREAK ROOM — DAY

Darla sits at the table covering her face with her hands, Dan sits next to her. The TV plays the news.

DAN

Take a day off and catch up on the sleep. Okay?

Darla just nods her head quietly.

DAN

Oh, and Finny says he feels like he's cheating you if he doesn't pay you something for that phone call.

She slaps him playfully. She is laughing so hard she can't make a sound.

DARLA

Thanks, Dan. I'm sorry.

DAN

Don't mention it. We're all tired.

The TV catches his eye as Darla gets up and leaves. He turns it up.

TV VO

...today at the court house. The Porters — owners of The Stetson nightclub — in their third court appearance this year, maintain that the anonymous tips have no basis in fact. When leaving the building, older brother Kyle Porter wore his characteristic smug grin and refused to answer any questions. Authorities say...

DAN

Nah, couldn't be.

INT — 7-11 — NIGHT

Dan is at the counter with a cup of coffee talking with WENDY the cashier.

WENDY

Working graveyard tonight, Dan?

DAN

No, I just need to smack some employees

on the forehead before things get out
of hand.

                    WENDY

Sounds like a fun night.

                    DAN

Psssh. Those two are gonna kill me.

                    WENDY

Take it easy, huh?

EXT — 7-11 PARKING LOT — NIGHT

Dan shuffles toward Kopy King when he spots TREY
standing next to a FANCY CAR parked next to him.

                    TREY

Hey City Boy. Ya'll need a lift?

Dan scrutinizes him, unsure wtf.

                    DAN

No man, I'm good, I work right here. But
thanks for asking.

Trey moves his jacket revealing a gun. He snears.

                    TREY

I wasn't askin', Chato.

A car door opens. Trey shoves Dan in and climbs in
after; the car takes off.

INT — FANCY CAR — NIGHT

Dan is wedged between TREY and KYLE PORTER, mean
looking guys in nice suits and big hats. Kyle just
stares ahead while he talks.

                    KYLE

Dan Sommers?

Dan stares at them.

                    KYLE

The employees working graveyard said you
were the one to talk to if we had issues
with our order.

                    DAN

If this is someone's idea of giving me a
surprise promotion, I'll take it.

Trey punches Dan in the stomach.

>   TREY
>
>   If'n it ain't you, we can find who it is.

Dan uncurls from the punch and looks up.

>   DAN
>
>   Oh shit. You guys are the Porter's,
>   aren't you. Seen your face in the
>   papers, TV a couple of times.

>   TREY
>
>   Yeah, boy! We get acquitted a lot.

Kyle gives Trey a look.

>   DAN
>
>   I'm the one to talk to. Why?

>   KYLE
>
>   It's like this, partner: we seem to have
>   new legal action directed at us, fueled
>   by letters received from an anonymous
>   source... which was traced back to your
>   store.

>   DAN
>
>   I don't know what you're talking about.

Trey belts Dan, he doubles up.

>   TREY
>
>   That jog your memory, cowboy?

>   DAN
>
>   Okay... okay okay. It's taken care of.

>   KYLE
>
>   You are a smart feller. You learn fast.
>   So listen up hombre. Rattlers get their
>   heads blowed off and made into boots. You
>   need to hear that, Cause you about to
>   come outta the chute on an angry Brahma,
>   and you gonna get throwed in the sawdust
>   in way under 8 seconds and stomped so
>   hard your own momma won't know which end
>   is up. Comprende?

                    DAN

        Uhhhh... yes?

                    TREY

        Good. Don't make us drive into town
        again.

Trey roughs up Dan a few more times.

The car screeches to a halt back at the 7-11.

EXT — 7-11 — NIGHT

The door opens and Dan is tossed out, still holding his
coffee. The car speeds off.

                    DAN

        Okay... things are officially out of
        hand.

INT — PRINTSHOP PRODUCTION ROOM — NIGHT

Dan walks in and sees Pip and Sarah copying their faces
on the color copier. There are no customers in the
store.

                    SARAH

        Dan, what happened to you, you look like
        hell?

Dan does not answer. He walks quickly over to where
they are and slams the copier cover down on Pip, and
smacks Sarah on her forehead.

                    PIP

        Ow!

                    SARAH

        Dude, what happened?!

                    DAN

        Your buddies, the Porters, just snagged
        me and were seriously convinced that
        somebody in my store — cause I'm the
        manager, you know — has been tipping
        the cops on their actions, which were in
        highly confidential documents that
        we copied.

                    SARAH

        What?

Sarah and Pip hang their heads.

> DAN
>
> Are you batshit insane? I'd ask if you were high, but I know better.

> PIP
>
> We're sorry, Dan.

> DAN
>
> Not as sorry as my bruised spleen, Pip. What were you guys thinking?

> SARAH
>
> We're sick to death of their condescending little faces every time they get off, man. They break the law, and every single time they get off.

> PIP
>
> And we get busted for having a little recreational agriculture in our cars.

> DAN
>
> Guys, I haven't sold my book yet, and I really want to live to see that. Knock it off. Do NOT write any more letters to the COPS. You dig me?

They nod after a moment.

Dan holds his ribs and wanders out.

> SARAH
>
> Bastards.

> PIP
>
> They fucking with the wrong people now.

INT — PRINTSHOP PRODUCTION ROOM — DAY

Antoinette enters and glances around the store. Brad picks up a package and intercepts her.

> BRAD
>
> Miss Duquesne? I have your order here.

She is slightly startled, but takes the package and sets it down on the counter.

                    BRAD

     I finally took care of the problem my-
     self. I noticed Finny had been running
     it on the wrong color paper and had not
     checked to make sure the back side lined
     up with the front on the folds.

Antoinette takes out a sample and looks it over.

                  ANTOINETTE

     You ran it... correctly.

                    BRAD

     Yes ma'am.

Antoinette flips through the stack.

Finny enters from the back. Darla and Mike both see the
storm approaching.

Finny sees Brad with Antoinette and stops dead.

                  ANTOINETTE

     What the hell did you do?

                    BRAD

     What did I...? I'm new here, and even I
     could tell that he had no idea what he
     was doing.

                  ANTOINETTE

     You made it all come out right. You ruin
     it.

                    BRAD

     What?

                  ANTOINETTE

     Where is your manager? I want to speak
     with your manager.

                    BRAD

     You're upset? Are you nuts?

Antoinette sees Finny and motions to him.

                  ANTOINETTE

     Stuart, there you are! Why did you
     let this stupid man touch my order? I
     thought you were taking care of me?

Finny hurries over to the counter as Brad backs off in
complete bewilderment.

                    FINNY

        I'm sorry, Antoinette, I don't...

                    ANTOINETTE

        How could you do this to me? I'm gone
        for one week and someone else is jump in
        and mess with our project?

                    FINNY

        Really, I have no idea what happened,
        but I will definitely...

                    BRAD

        You people are insane.

Brad shakes his head and throws up his hands as he
heads for the back.

Antoinette throws down the papers and turns to leave.

                    ANTOINETTE

        You don't care about me. No more I will
        come here. Goodbye.

                    FINNY

        Please let me take care of you. I'll
        personally deliver it to your office, is
        that alright?

                    ANTOINETTE

        (Over her shoulder) Yes. Fine. But de-
        liver it to my house, I no work today.

Finny watches her go, then glances over his shoulder
and fumes toward Brad, who drinks a cup of water. Finny
flips him off and gives him an insincere smile.

                    BRAD

        Tool.

Maggie comes in the back door, and she and Brad start
to talk. The smile fades from Finny's face.

Dan watches Maggie and Brad being chatty at the back of
the room as he drills paper. Finny approaches Dan with
a package.

                    FINNY

          Hey, Dan. The new shrink wrapper just
          came in, what do we do with it.

Dan doesn't turn his gaze away from Maggie and Brad.
Smoke starts to waft up from the paper.

Finny stands there for a moment. Dan turns to him
finally.

                    DAN

          I don't know, what DO we DO with a
          shrink wrapper, Finny? Here's a thought:
          Open the god damn thing, set it up, and
          have graveyard shrink-wrap shit with it.
          Jesus, figure it out.

Dan shoves the smoking ream at Finny. It is burned
around the holes. Dan storms away. Finny looks over at
Brad being touchy feely with Maggie.

EXT — MOVIE THEATER — NIGHT

Maggie and Brad exit and walk to the parking lot.

                    BRAD

          Hey, that movie was pretty good. That
          Stallone — he is still so awesome!

                    MAGGIE

          Yeah. What I was thinking.

                    BRAD

          You watch a lot of TV and movies?

                    MAGGIE

          No. Not really. Don't have ti...

                    BRAD

          Oh, me neither. (pause) Jeez, there's so
          much to do in this town.

Maggie motions down the street.

                    MAGGIE

          Uh, there's a coffee joint — near here I
          think... Dan loves it.

                    BRAD

          Meh, ok.

They walk down the street.

EXT — COFFEE SHOP — NIGHT

A "Closed" sign hangs on the door; pictures can be seen in the windows.

                              MAGGIE

          Oh, it's closed. I guess I should have
          checked. Dan would have known.

                              BRAD

          That's okay, it's kind of nice out here
          anyway.

                              MAGGIE

          Yeah, it is.

She looks up at the moon, then back at a painting in the window.

                              MAGGIE

          Dan said he went to Mexico once and
          there was a place like this, where you
          could swim with Dolphins.

                              BRAD

          Dan. What a lunk-head.

                              MAGGIE

          He has his moments.

                              BRAD

          He's so overbearing and self-absorbed. I
          can't stand the way...

Maggie gives him a look, he's pushing it.

                              BRAD

          Hey, I heard there's a bar with a
          mechanical bull. Is it close?

She looks at Brad rather blankly.

                              MAGGIE

          Yeah. Look, I need to run by the store
          real quick. You mind?

                              BRAD

          Ok, no problem.

INT — PRINTSHOP PRODUCTION ROOM — NIGHT

Maggie enters and sees Sarah with a customer.

Pip is shrink-wrapping one of the registers. There are quite a few things wrapped, including pencil cups, staplers and phones.

                         PIP

          Hey Maggie

                        MAGGIE

          Hey Pip. Seen Dan?

                         PIP

          Nah. He split with second shift.

                        MAGGIE

          Everything okay?

Pip and Sarah catch each other's gaze for a second.

                         PIP

          Yeah Everything's cool. Hey, you got a
          message from Abe. It's in your office.

Maggie goes to her office.

INT — MAGGIE'S OFFICE — NIGHT

Maggie picks up the message from her desk and reads.

                        MAGGIE

          "Coming in Monday with big news. Abe."

The phone rings, she grabs it. The entire phone, rest and all, is shrink-wrapped. The call is answered outside.

                        MAGGIE

          Jesus. Pip...

She looks at the phone, then rips it open and dials. She hangs up and stares at the phone.

INT — PRINTSHOP PRODUCTION ROOM — NIGHT

Maggie comes out of the back and sees Brad talking to Sarah and Pip. They are all laughing.

                        MAGGIE

          Hey Brad, I'm sorry. I'm ready to go
          now. Can you wait outside a minute, I
          gotta talk some shop?

                         BRAD

          Sure. See you guys later.

He leaves. Sarah and Pip smile as Brad leaves, then
lose their phony grins as soon as he is gone.

                        MAGGIE

          Hey guys, have you noticed...

                        SARAH

          What a douche.

                         PIP

          Total douche.

                        MAGGIE

          (confused) What?

                        SARAH

          You'd think a guy who played a global
          adventurer would be cooler.

                      MAGGIE/PIP

          (both confused now) What?

                        SARAH

          Duh. That's Brad Mitchell from "Jungle
          Force."

                         PIP

          No it isn't.

                        SARAH

          The hell it ain't.

                        MAGGIE

          His name is Brad Mann.

                        SARAH

          Maggie, I have cable, I get every chan-
          nel on the planet. Early in the morn-
          ing they show reruns of Jungle Force. He
          played the young Indiana Jones rip-off.

Maggie looks toward the door then back at Sarah.

                        SARAH

          Watch the show. 8 am on TV Land.

> PIP

That show sucked. Dick.

> SARAH

Everything he's ever done sucks dick. I guess that's why he's working here.

Maggie thinks about it, then leaves.

INT — MAGGIE'S CAR — NIGHT

Maggie glances at Brad as she drives.

> BRAD

Seriously, Maggie, if I was Brad Mitchell, why would I be working in a copy shop?

> MAGGIE

You tell me. She seemed real sure.

> BRAD

Right. It's such an awesome show I'm throwing it away to make stupid copies.

> MAGGIE

She said the show sucked.

> BRAD

It didn't suck. It was pretty good. The guy who was in it... just got a role in a film... I heard.

> MAGGIE

I can look it up.

> BRAD

(Using his liar voice) So? Look it up. I can't help it if I look like some other guy. What's with the second degree all the sudden? It won't mean anything.

> MAGGIE

I'm pretty tired, Brad, I hope you don't mind.

> BRAD

No, that's cool. We should get some sleep. Can't function without sleep. Your place or mine?

He wiggles his eyebrows up and down, Maggie rolls her
eyes.

INT — PRINTSHOP PRODUCTION ROOM — DAY

Dan, looking disheveled and unshaven, walks in from the
street. Finny waves to him from the counter.

> FINNY
>
> Hey man, how's it going?

Dan grumbles incoherently.

> FINNY
>
> That was harsh, even for a Monday.

Dan goes around the counter and is stopped by a LADY at
the computer services center.

> COMPUTER LADY
>
> Excuse me, do you work here? I need to
> get logged onto a computer.

Dan doesn't break stride. He walks straight to the
computer, angrily logs her on with heavy key strokes,
and leaves.

> COMPUTER LADY
>
> Um, thank you.

INT — PRINTSHOP BREAK ROOM — DAY

Dan checks mail/messages, chucks the pile across the
room as Barry comes out of the bathroom.

> BARRY
>
> Morning boss. How was your weekend?

Dan glares at Barry.

> BARRY
>
> Eeeewwwww.

Barry watches Dan stomp to the office.

INT — PRINTSHOP PRODUCTION ROOM — DAY

Maggie walks with a purpose through the front of the
store. She sees Barry.

> MAGGIE
>
> Hey, Barry. Is Dan here?

                         BARRY

        Yeah, he's in the office, but I wouldn't
        go in there if I were you.

Maggie whizzes past him and goes to the office.

                         MAGGIE

        Well, you're not me, and it's killing
        you.

                         BARRY

        Meowrrr.

INT — MAGGIE'S OFFICE — DAY

Maggie throws open the door and sees Dan sprawled
asleep on the desk.

                         MAGGIE

        Dan. Okay, I'm sorry, you were right.
        And also I just want to say...

Dan doesn't stir. Maggie looks at him, he seems so worn
out. She touches his hand.

                         MAGGIE

                 Dan?

Dan jumps awake and stares around bleary
eyed.

                         DAN

        What? What? I made the service call this
        morning!

                         MAGGIE

        (playfully) You're supposed to sleep at
        home, silly.

Dan runs his hands through his hair and yawns.

                         DAN

        (angrily) If you ever let me go home.

                         MAGGIE

        What?

Dan sits back in the chair, trying to wake up.

                         DAN

        I'm sorry, am I grunting again?

                    MAGGIE

No. I...

                    DAN

You... got me working damn near three
shifts because you think just because
you have no life NOBODY has one.

                    MAGGIE

What are you talking about?

                    DAN

I understand you're worried about the
new owners and what they'll think. And
I understand that this is a really busy
time. But the thing that really gets me,
is that instead of working more yourself, you're out prancing around with
that fucktard.

                    MAGGIE

So that's what this has all been about?
You're jealous?

Dan mumbles.

                    MAGGIE

What is it with you men and... what is
it with you damn men?

                    DAN

And what is it with you damn women? Some
pretty boy comes in here with no skills
or character, and you go gaga over him
instantly. The whole time you're saying
how "looks don't matter..."

Maggie starts to answer and stops several times. Some
of the employees are peeking through the doorway.

                    DAN

Yeah, great come back, Maggie. What's
the matter, run out of words to put in
my mouth? Or are you too tired after
making out with Brad all weekend while
the rest of us were covering your ass?

                    MAGGIE

Get out.

                    DAN

     Good. I'm out.

                  MAGGIE

     Fine. Go.

                    DAN

     Gone. You gonna hire three male dancers
     to replace me.

                  MAGGIE

     You're fired, Sommers, get the hell OUT.

She turns and almost runs into Abe, who is standing in
the doorway wide-eyed.

                    ABE

     Well, this isn't what I expected.

Dan storms past Abe.

                    DAN

     Hey Abe, Just in time. Your princess has
     turned into a toad.

                    ABE

     What's going on?

                  MAGGIE

     Dan was just leaving.

                    ABE

     Come on guys, let's talk about this.

Abe moves sits in a chair. He is a little shaken.

                  MAGGIE

     Stay out of this Abe. It's between Dan
     and I.

                    DAN

     Dan and me.

                  MAGGIE

     Shut up, Sommers.

                    DAN

     Make me, McCallister.

                    ABE

          Cut it out already. What happened? I
          thought you two...

                    DAN

          Me? And Her? PLEASE.

                    MAGGIE

          That's because you're too in love with
          yourself.

                    DAN

          At least I have time for me, and I take
          me out for some fun, instead of asking
          myself to work eighteen hours a day...

                    MAGGIE

          I'm surprised you're not jealous of
          yourself for spending so much time
          with you.

                    DAN

          No, I'm a lot easier to take than you,
          Dragon Lady.

                    MAGGIE

          Dragon Lady? Kiss my ass.

                    DAN

          Get Brad to, McCallister. You fired me,
          remember?

He storms out the back and slams the door. Maggie
stares after him a minute, then turns to Abe, not
really looking at him.

                    MAGGIE

          Can you believe that insufferable... I
          came in here to tell him that I was...
          oooh he just makes me... I want to grab
          him and...

She looks at Abe, who is having trouble breathing and
is sweating.

                    MAGGIE

          Abe? Are you alright? Abe?

She kneels beside him and calls out the door.

                    MAGGIE

          Barry? Somebody, call 911!

Everyone scrambles.

                    MAGGIE

          Stay with me Abe.

                     ABE

          My chest hurts… oh man.

INT — HOSPITAL WAITING ROOM — NIGHT

A doctor approaches Maggie, who sits on a couch.

                    DOCTOR

          Ms. McCallister?

                    MAGGIE

          Yes. How is he?

                    DOCTOR

          He's alright. His heart is fine, but a
          poorly timed muscle spasm. And a lot of
          gas. Anxiety attack we think, anyway it
          kind of snowballed. We're going to move
          him to a room, keep him overnight to
          make sure.

                    MAGGIE

          Can I see him?

                    DOCTOR

          Sure, he asked for you, go on in.

                    MAGGIE

          Thank you.

She hurries out of the waiting room.

INT — ABE'S HOSPITAL ROOM — NIGHT

Abe lies in bed, watches TV, looks uncomfortable.
He farts.

                    MAGGIE

          Hey Abe. You okay?

                     ABE

          Am I okay? You and Dan gave me a near
          fatal heart attack, and you call that

>   okay? Doctor says another one could kill
>   me.
>
>   MAGGIE
>
>   You're fine.
>
>   ABE
>
>   I'm fine?
>
>   MAGGIE
>
>   The doctor said... look, I'm Sorry.
>
>   ABE
>
>   What was that all about, kid? I thought
>   you two were good together?
>
>   MAGGIE
>
>   I don't know about that.
>
>   ABE
>
>   He's in love with you, dumbass. What are
>   you, blind?
>
>   MAGGIE
>
>   No. I'm not, I'm, I'm...
>
>   ABE
>
>   Stupid?
>
>   MAGGIE
>
>   Yes.
>
>   ABE
>
>   Don't end up like me, kid. The name of
>   the store is "Kopy King," not "Maggie's
>   Copies." Don't let it ruin your life.
>
>   MAGGIE
>
>   But...
>
>   ABE
>
>   I sold my shares before they could shove
>   me out. I bought myself a nice little
>   low-stress business and I'm gonna have
>   fun for the years I got left.
>
>   MAGGIE
>
>   But who...

                    ABE

    Who gives a fiddling fart, kid? It's a
    job. Put in your hours. Do your best.
    Pick up your check. Go home. HAVE A
    LIFE. Repeat as necessary.

Maggie just stares at him

                    ABE

    I'm glad we had this talk. Hey, go
    get me one of those great calzones
    from Pizzo's.

                    MAGGIE

    You hate those calzones.

                    ABE

    I've looked at death's bony, emaciated
    face... I love everything.

                    DOCTOR

    (walking past) It was gas, Abe.
    Drama much?

                    ABE

    Ooh, look here, you see this?

He uses the remote to turn up the volume on the TV.

                    TV VO

    ... in January. Again, our top story,
    The Stetson Club owners Trey and Kyle
    Porter have mysteriously disappeared.
    They were last seen meeting with family
    members on Saturday...

                    ABE

    Some family. My guess is their godfather
    got tired of their high profile. About
    time somebody nailed their asses.

INT — PRINTSHOP PRODUCTION ROOM — DAY

Maggie enters and all the employees' heads turn toward
her. They are not happy. She smiles weakly and heads to
the counter.

                    FINNY

    So Mike, you hear what happened to Abe?

                    MIKE

        Yeah. Almost died.

                    FINNY

        Yep. Right after... you know.

They glare at Maggie, who goes to help Mrs.
Wolfenhaber.

Darla turns from her customer to Maggie.

                    DARLA

        Oh. YOU'RE here. There's a service call
        on the 9500. Spots.

She turns quickly away.

                    MAGGIE

        It's just the belt, Dan can clean...

Everyone scowls. Barry lets out a stifled cry.

                MRS. WOLFENHABER

        Where is Dan? I haven't seen him in a
        few days.

                    MAGGIE

        Oh, he's uh, he,

Finny steps up and puts some new pens in a cup.

                    FINNY

        He's not here anymore. Fired.

                MRS. WOLFENHABER

        What kind of turdball fires Dan? Did Kopy
        King sell out to Fascists?

                    MAGGIE

        No. I'm not a, I mean, the person that
        fired him didn't sell-out, he was ...it
        was his fault, really. I don't look at
        his ass, he's got hands, too. Stupid
        jungle-man anyway, I don't even like
        him. It's not Fascists, it's jealous
        writers.

She looks around for a sympathetic face amongst her
coworkers. Her mind starts to play tricks on her.

                    MIKE

          Finny, this job for Dandridge is ready.

                    FINNY

          Dandy. I'll QC it.

                    DARLA

          The Dance club called from up stairs.
          They need more tickets.

                    FINNY

          Dan it, this box is danaged.

                    MRS. WOLFENHABER

          I need a copy of this china pattern.
          It's Blue Danube.

Barry is on the intercom.

                    BARRY VO

             Dan, phone call on line dan, Dan, line
             dan.

Maggie looks at the high speed copier chugging out
copies, it makes a sound like dandandandandan.

                    MAGGIE

             STOP IT. Stop it already, I fired him,
             okay? It was me, alright. I shit-canned
             him. It was all my fault. Now leave me
             alone already. There, under the floor
             boards, it's his hideous beating heart!

Silence.

Employees and customers stare at Maggie, who wrings the
hell out of one of Mrs. Wolfenhaber's photos.

                    MAGGIE

             Oh! I'm so sorry, Mrs. Wolfenhaber, um,
             let me fix this.

She tries to flatten out the photo but it crumples.
Maggie tries to glue it and tape it but makes a mess.

                    MRS. WOLFENHABER

             That's my grandmother.

                    MAGGIE

          She was very pretty. She has a lot of

> wrinkles. The picture does, not her. Oh,
> I did that, sorry.

Barry gently puts an arm around Maggie and leads her
away from the counter.

                    BARRY

> Come on, Maggie, let's sit you down in
> the office. Finny?

Finny helps Mrs. Wolfenhaber.

INT — MAGGIE'S OFFICE — DAY

Barry Sits Maggie down at the desk.

                    MAGGIE

> I don't know what to do, Barry.

                    BARRY

> I think you know what to do, girl.
> You're a wreck. Take some time. Relax.

                    MAGGIE

> I can't relax. There's too much work,
> and... and... I don't know how.

                    BARRY

What?

                    MAGGIE

> This is what I do, I've been here twelve
> years... I don't know how to relax. I'm
> too tired to sleep... I...

Barry looks out the door and back to her.

                    BARRY

> You didn't get this from me.

He walks to the file cabinet and opens the bottom
drawer, pulls it nearly out of the cabinet, then
reaches under it and pulls something out.

                    MAGGIE

> What is that?

                    BARRY

> Study guide.

He flops the thing on the desk. It is Sarah and Pip's
bag of pot with the pink bow. Maggie raise an eyebrow.

INT — PRINTSHOP PRODUCTION ROOM — DAY

Finny and Darla glance toward the office.

> DARLA
>
> She's been in there a long time. Think she's okay?

> FINNY
>
> Maybe you should check.

> DARLA
>
> You check.

> FINNY
>
> Not me. They might be doing girl stuff.

> DARLA
>
> You're a dunce.

Darla approaches the door and goes to knock.

Barry emerges and quickly pulls the door shut behind him. A cloud of smoke wafts out from the office.

> BARRY
>
> Maggie will be taking the day off.

INT — MAGGIE'S APT — DAY

Maggie sits at her coffee table eating junk food. There is a knock at the door, she gets up slowly and answers it. It's Brad, he comes in.

> BRAD
>
> Hey. What's up?

> MAGGIE
>
> Remember when I had trouble hiring you?

> BRAD
>
> Yes. Why?

> MAGGIE
>
> Cause I'm not having any trouble saying you're fired.

> BRAD
>
> What? Why?

                    MAGGIE

          Because you're a creep, a liar, a
          douchebag... and a really bad actor.

                    BRAD

          It's... not me.

                    MAGGIE

          Give me a break, do I look stupid?

She has crumbs and frosting on her face.

                    MAGGIE

          I looked you up online. They said you
          were researching a movie role by working
          at some "menial, customer service job"
          in Texas. What do you say to that?

Brad tries to think up something, but can't. He lets
out a breathy laugh.

                    BRAD

          Doesn't matter now, I got what I need,
          thanks. You people are better than any
          screenplay.

                    MAGGIE

          I'm glad we're so interesting to you.
          Get lost.

Brad laughs, gets up and walks out. He turns back
toward Maggie.

                    BRAD

          Sure you don't want to go have one last
          dinner? You've earned it. I have a
          friend who's a chef.

                    MAGGIE

          No thanks, Farm-boy. I've got my own
          chef.

She brandishes a can of Chef Boyardee. Brad smirks and
leaves.

                    MAGGIE

          I'm not stupid. I can see stuff.

She stuffs more ravioli into her mouth, washing it down
with a mango cooler.

                    MAGGIE

     So Dan likes me, who didn't see that?

She tosses the fork into the can and drops the can on
the table. She grabs her hair and growls.

                    MAGGIE

     Arrg! I'm such a dickhead.

She picks up her phone, stares at it a second, then
hangs up.

She picks up again and dials. She hears the operator
informing her that the number is not working.

INT — PRINTSHOP PRODUCTION ROOM — NIGHT

Maggie and Barry sit at Barry's desk.

                    MAGGIE

     I can't find him. I've tried calling, but
     his phone is out. He doesn't answer his
     door either.

                    BARRY

     He's just blowing off steam, Maggie. I'm
     sure he'll show up, give him some time.

Finny wanders over to them.

                    FINNY

     Abe said he'll be ready to go in a few
     minutes. Hey — You guys hear about the
     Porters?

                    MAGGIE

No.

                    BARRY

     Found them in a drainage ditch on a farm
     road in Bastrop.

                    MAGGIE

No shit?

                    FINNY

     Sarah and Pip wrote to their "board of
     directors," told them how sloppy things
     were being handled here in Austin.

                    MAGGIE

    Dan told those guys to knock it off.

                    FINNY

    Technically, he said "stop writing the
    cops."

Finny starts to look at himself in a mirror, coming his
hair with his fingers, adjusting his shirt.

Maggie watches Finny primping. He's humming.

                    MAGGIE

    Got a date or something, Finny?

                    FINNY

    Yes ma'am.

                    BARRY

    Really? You?

                    FINNY

    Yes ma'am.

                    MAGGIE

    Gonna tell us who it is?

Before Finny can answer, we hear Antoinette's voice
from the door way.

                    ANTOINETTE

    Stuart? Why are you not ready yet? I
    said eight thirty.

Finny turns. Antoinette is nicely dressed. He can't
think of anything to say.

                    ANTOINETTE

    What are you waiting for? Let's go.

Finny rushes away from the mirror.

                    FINNY

    I'm sorry, ma'am... I mean Antoinette.
    Let me get my... I'll be right out. I'm
    sorry.

He runs to the back, untying his apron.

                    ANTOINETTE

    Thank you for letting him off early,
    Maggie.

Maggie raises an eyebrow, looks at Barry.

                    MAGGIE

          I did that?

Barry just nods.

                    MAGGIE

          No problem. Have fun.

                    ANTOINETTE

          We will.

Finny rushes back out and heads for the door.

                    FINNY

          Man, I'm so sorry I'm late, it won't
          happen again.

He rushes ahead and opens the door for Antoinette. She
turns to Maggie and smiles

                    ANTOINETTE

          He is SO sexy!

Antoinette and Finny leave. Maggie watches through the
windows as they turn the corner arm in arm.

                    BARRY

          Guess I'm out too — karaoke tonight at
          the show. Why don't you come by?

He gets up to leave, Maggie looks around the store,
then turns to check a job on the QC table.

                    MAGGIE

          (flatly) Yeah. Maybe. Have a good night,
          Barry.

She spots Mike at the back, he gives her an awkward
smile and waves. She hears the door open, Mrs.
Wolfenhaber's enters.

                    MRS. WOLFENHABER

          Maggie? Is Abe here?

Maggie turns and sees Mrs. Wolfenhaber all dolled up.

                    MAGGIE

          He's in the back, Mrs. Wolfenhaber, get-
          ting ready for... a... date?

It dawns on her.

                    MAGGIE

          You and Mr. Spinetti?

Mrs. Wolfenhaber just smiles and gives a quick nod.

                 MRS. WOLFENHABER

          We found out we had a lot in common. So
          we decided to make up for lost time.

Abe comes in from the back hall.

                     ABE

          Connie, you're here already. God damn
          it.

                    MAGGIE

          Your first date in fifty years and that's
          the best you can do?

                     ABE

          No, It's this damn tie, I've been trying
          to tie it for the last twenty minutes.
          Who the Hell came up with this bullshit,
          the Marquis de Sade?

                 MRS. WOLFENHABER

          Never mind Abe, you look great the way
          you are.

                     ABE

          My kind of woman, Connie. I'm throwing
          away all my ties. Both of them. Come on
          back, I've got something for you.

Mrs. Wolfenhaber smiles and follows Abe back.

Maggie watches them go and lets out a long sigh, then
grumpily continues her work.

                    MAGGIE

          I am so glad everybody is having such a
          god damn good time.

She looks back at Mike... he is unsure what to do with
her look. Another voice interrupts her.

                     VOICE

          Can I get a couple copies of this book,
          bounded, by tomorrow.

Maggie turns, grabs a pen and a job ticket, and writes without looking up. She looks at the book.

                    MAGGIE

          I'm sorry, we can't duplicate this sir,
          it's copyrighted material.

                    MAN

          It's okay, I'm the author.

Maggie looks closely at the cover. She sees the name Dan Sommers. She looks up at Dan standing sheepishly.

                    MAGGIE

          "Together" by Dan Sommers. Prometheus
          Publishing. Holy crap.

                    DAN

          I know, right? Got a FedEx package with
          a contract. They flew me to New York to
          meet the editor.

                    MAGGIE

Oh my gosh, Dan. Holy crap.

                    DAN

          A: you already said that, and B: Thank
          you. (off Maggie's look) Read the dedica-
          tion.

Maggie turns it over and sees a picture of Dan in a Kopy King sweatshirt. She smiles and opens to the dedication.

                    MAGGIE

          I need to thank my best friend in the
          whole world for making this, my first
          novel, possible through her undying
          friendship, and unrelenting support...
          not to mention all the free copies. Mag-
          gie McCallister, Manager at Kopy King in
          Austin, TX.

She shakes her head, stifling a tear. They stand there in silence until Abe's voice breaks it up.

                    ABE

          You both going to stand there all frig-
          gin' night, or are you going to get on
          with your lives?

Abe and Connie stand behind them smiling. Connie wears
a corsage.

                    ABE

          Come on, I'm buying... let's all go get
          a burger at Hut's, and then go sing gay
          karaoke.

Abe waves to Mike at the folder.

                    ABE

          Hey, Nature Boy, watch the store. Feel
          free to express yourself.

Mike looks to Maggie and Dan, in shock.

                    MIKE

          Is this a trap? You have to tell me if
          you're a cop.

Abe makes a face of intense confusion.

                    ABE

          What kind of trap...? How does one...

                    MAGGIE

          Let it all hang out, Mike.

She walks around to Dan with a stern look.

                    MAGGIE

          I guess you think I'm just going to dump
          my job now and follow you around to book
          signings, huh?

                    DAN

          I kinda thought you'd let me come back
          to work so I can start on my next one.

                    MAGGIE

          Who cares what you think?

Dan tears up, fights it back... a little

                    DAN

          If it were only you and no one else, I'd
          be really happy.

Maggie completely breaks down in tears.

                    MAGGIE

     It takes you years to say something, and
     all you can do is make me cry?

They kiss, Maggie wipes her eyes on his shirt. Dan
wipes his eyes on her apron.

                      ABE

     Good God... are they BOTH crying?

                 MRS. WOLFENHABER

     Stop it, it's sweet.

Maggie dumps her apron on the counter.

Mike fiddles with the stereo and soon we hear Texas
flavored rock throughout the store. Abe and Connie head
for the door.

                      ABE

     Connie, we need to get that book of
     yours published. Did I tell you that I
     just bought Prometheus Publishing?

                 MRS. WOLFENHABER

     Really? They've published some great
     writers.

                      ABE

     Some of the best.

They leave the store, followed by Dan and Maggie.

We pan back across the room. The music is in full
swing, Mike is working hard, folding and packing
letters, playing air guitar and lip-synching.

He is also completely naked.

FADE OUT

FADE IN

INT — PRODUCTION ROOM — EVENING

Jerry walks in with a box of materials, Mike waves
wildly at him from the counter.

                      MIKE

     HEY! Jerry!

Jerry just stares, drops his box of stuff all over the
floor.

                    JERRY
          Oh, for fuck's sake.

FADE OUT

THE END

COMICS AND ROBBERS

I love Improv.

I discovered it in the early 80s in Las Vegas, when it really did not have much of a presence there at all. I was doing stand-up in college, and the comics I used to hang out with turned me onto it. A few of us started a troupe called Nine Pin. At the time, I was the youngest member, 18. The oldest member was a comic/actor named Joe, who was in his 70s I think. He mostly did roles as a gangsters in movies... but was actually rather funny on stage.

We did maybe one or two shows at some open-mic-type events before things fell apart, and I went back to plain-old stand-up. I took a few years off to help raise kids, and in 1992 I got a bug up my ass to do comedy again. We had just moved to Austin, and I tried stand-up for a short time, but fell in love with the thriving improv scene.

I met some comics in a film acting workshop – they did not care much for the highly organized improv troupes that were getting franchised across the country – and we started a group called Monks' Night Out in the mid 90s. We set our first show date for the predicted Doomsday that was supposed to occur late September 1994, according to prophet Harold Camping. No Doomsday, but we hit the stage with a BAM. About a year later, we were getting pretty well-known, and had even gotten ourselves voted Best Theater Company by an *Austin Chronicle* Poll.

I loved the whole vibe that improv offered, the surge of adrenaline that came from stepping onto stage with nothing really rehearsed and nailed down. Playing with that energy was a rush. We also wove some short sketches into the mix, which I was happy to write, and later more and more cast members wrote as well.

There was an extra excitement one year when we heard that some scouts were coming to check out our show with an eye on maybe using us in the US version of *Whose Line Is It Anyway*. That never panned out, but man, was that cool to be in the running for as long as it lasted.

The troupe worked really well together, and those first few years were the best times ever, even on the nights when joke after joke, bit after bit, hit the floor like a lead balloon and even the crickets were keeping quiet.

I left the troupe a few years later, as I was getting more and more acting work that took up all my time, and I couldn't afford to take any more attention away from family. I knew there was a screenplay in there somewhere, and when I read some story in a newspaper about a ridiculous bank robbery attempt somewhere, it all clicked together for me.

I never did much with *Comics and Robbers*, it was a bit esoteric for most contests I guess, and likely a logistical nightmare for movie producers. I kinda knew that going in, comics being what they are. But I still get a kick out of reading it every couple years, and the memories it brings back are priceless.

Darkness. Sounds of clinking glasses, laughter and live keyboard music. Voices start to speak, quick and campy.

                    WOMAN

        Hi, do you come here often?

                    MAN 1

        No, no. I just need to use the phone, I
        had an accident outside.

                    WOMAN

        Oh, What happened?

                    MAN 1

        Well, my car hit a walrus that had es-
        caped from the zoo across the street
        there, and its tusk seems to have gotten
        wedged in my ass, see?

                    WOMAN

        Oh my God!

                    MAN 2

        FREEZE!

Sounds of laughter and snickering, rapid movement.

                    WOMAN

        You're it!

                    MAN 2

Wow, that is the coolest jet-pack I have
ever seen. How does it work?

                    MAN 1

I'm not sure, I found it at a rummage
sale. Can you believe it, forty bucks?

                    MAN 2

What does that tag right there say?

                    MAN 1

Oh, the directions. It looks like you
just press this button here and...
WHOAAAAA!

                  WOMAN 2

FREEZE!

Again, movement and sounds of an appreciative audience.

                    MAN 2

You're it.

                    MAN 3

Oh, Marsha... I love you. Tell me that
you love me too.

                  WOMAN 2

I'd like to, Jerry, but I can't. For,
you see...

                    MAN 3

No, Don't say it!

                  WOMAN 2

But I must. I am already married — and
have a child.

                    MAN 3

No, no, no!

                  WOMAN 2

Yes! Look, I brought him with me. Here,
hold him, he loves it when you tickle
his...

                    MAN

FREEZE!

The performers themselves snicker, laughter from audience and rapid movement is heard once again, then a slap.

MAN 3

You are it!

FADE IN

INT — THEATER STAGE — EVENING

An AUDIENCE of about seventy to eighty people watches an improv show on a well-lit stage in a small theater. It is packed. The audience is laughing and having a good time.

Onstage are eight people. Two of them, MIKE STEFANIK, in his late twenties, friendly face; and SHARON MACINTIRE, in her thirties, voluptuous, a no-shit kind of woman, are front and center.

They stand with their hands out in front of them as if they are holding the same object.

MIKE

Oh, I'm sorry, was this your Homunculus?

SHARON

Yes it is. I found it at a rummage sale. Can you believe it, forty bucks!

They laugh at their own callback.

The rest of the CAST is in line at the back of the stage, each crouched in some manner of sprinter's stance.

Behind them the PICTURE of a cartoonish grandmother grins over the words GRANMA'S OUIJA BOARD.

SHARON

Can I have it back now, please?

MIKE

I guess so, where was it growing?

Mike stretches out his arms as if he is handing something large to Sharon.

SHARON

My neck, of course.

                         MIKE
        Well, let me put it back for you.

He starts to mime stuffing something large into her neck
and shoulder as her arms flail about.
                        SHARON

    Oooh! That tickles.

                         MIKE

        You know, what's really funny is I'll
        bet there's only a few people who actu-
        ally know what a Homunculus is, and none
        of them are in this room.

GIL PARDON, another member of the troupe, in his mid-
late thirties, shouts as he leaps forward.
                         GIL

    FREEZE!

The action immediately stops. Mike and Sharon hold
their poses, giggling. Gil steps forward and taps Mike
on the shoulder.
                         MIKE

        You're it!

Mike takes Gil's place in line. Gil takes the exact
same position that Mike held.
                         GIL

        Dang it all. There has got to be an eas-
        ier way to hang somebody.

He mimes trying to put a noose on Sharon as her arms
try to stave him off. Another member, TIFFANY CARSON,
a pretty young woman who is very well built, steps
forward

                        TIFFANY

        Hey there, pardner, Why don't you-all
        a-try tyin' her hands behind her, that
        aught'ta fix 'er.

Gil grudgingly mimes tying Sharon's hands behind her.
                         GIL

        Now how in hell is that supposed to...

He finishes the tying and Sharon now is completely still

with hands behind her. Gil pulls a "lever" and her head lolls to one side.

                          GIL

        Dang, it worked! Thanks, buddy.

He extends his arm to shake Tiffany's hand, which is right about crotch-high to Sharon, when STAN LUTHER, an angry-looking man in his late thirties, steps out from the line.

                         STAN

        FREEZE!

He comes forward and taps both Sharon and Gil.

                     GIL/TIFFANY

        You're it.

They move to the back of the stage. Stan takes up Sharon's position, then slowly raises his head smiling, as if awakening.

                        LUTHER

        Oh man! What an incredible orgasm. Now
        help me pull this gerbil out of my ass
        so you can try it.

The entire cast yells "Freeze!" all at the same time. The main lights on the stage go out and Loud applause and laughter is heard.

EXT — CITY STREET — DAY

Close on the marquee of THE GYPSY CART, the small cabaret in which we saw the previous scene. We move in through the front doors and pass the Granma's Ouija Board sign leaning up against a wall.

We HEAR some talking and laughter echoing in another room. We move through the inner doors and enter the main room. Mike Stefanik is on stage, and the six other members of the troupe sit on chairs and couches facing him.

                         MIKE

        Okay crybabies, "Tell me a joke" went
        way suck last night, so let's go over it
        one more time. When you ask for items
        from the audience, herd them toward the
        gimmees.

In the daylight the room is dingy and almost
depressing. The walls are covered with faux cracked
plaster on which are painted pictures of brightly
clothed Gypsies.

Mike gestures to the audience, in demonstration

                    MIKE

          Being comics, everybody's always com-
          ing up to us and saying "Tell me a joke,
          man." Well, we're gonna tell you a joke,
          and you'll supply the thing that the
          joke is about. It goes like this "A Nun,
          a Commie and a Blank are walking down
          the street, blah blah blah. May I have
          an item of clothing, please? Like some-
          thing a woman might wear, say, under her
          blouse but over her breasts?

One of the cast, TOMMY GEORGE, a short, funny-looking
kid in his twenties, half-assedly raises his hand.

                    TOMMY

     A bra

                    MIKE

     OK, the first thing I heard was "a bra,"
     thank you! I sure hope we can come up
     with a funny for that one! Ok, a Nun, a
     Commie and a Bra are walking down the
     street, a bum asks them for some cash.
     The commie says, "I do not believe in
     begging," and the Bra says "you'd bet-
     ter ask the sister here, cause I'm
     STRAPPED..."

This elicits groans from the other cast members in the
audience. Sharon raises her hand.

                    MIKE

     Yes, Sharon?

                    SHARON

     I've got an idea. Why don't we ask for
     things we really never get, and then...
     um, what's the term...

COLTON BLANKS cuts in from the bar. He is a slightly
overweight, bald kid in his late twenties.

                    COLTON

...make something up on the spur of the
moment?

                    SHARON

Yeah. Mike, uh, couldn't we just make
stuff up, like, on the spot?!

                    MIKE

Sorry, we're an Improv troupe, that
means we rehearse and rehearse and rehearse until we have our responses down
pat. What if we don't know any funny
jokes for "cordless phone?"

                    TOMMY

But, what if...

                    MIKE

...and if anyone doesn't like it,

He points to the back of the room, everyone joins him
on this part.

                    ALL

There's the fuckin' door!

                    MIKE

Now, let's try this again, let me get
everyone on stage and...

TIFFANY leans back in her chair and looks down the
hallway that leads past the stage. Something catches
her attention.

                    TIFFANY

Warning, Warning!

Without missing a beat, Mike shifts gears as Stan
enters from the hallway.

                    MIKE

So now that we did that exercise, let's
move on to...

                    LUTHER

Good to see everybody getting a little
extra practice in, we could use it after
last night.

They all start to gather around the foot of the stage.

                    TIFFANY

     What do you mean, Stan? That was a good
     show.

                    TOMMY

     Really. We killed last night.

                    LUTHER

     Yeah, Tommy, you're right. Except for
     the first ninety minutes, it was pretty
     good.

Gil rolls his eyes. He sits on a small loveseat near
the stage.

                    GIL

     Jesus.

                    LUTHER

     Just call me Stan, everyone else does,
     Gil. Seriously, we really need to work
     on "Tell me a Joke," so everyone up on
     stage. I don't know how many times I
     gotta tell you, go for the "gimmees,"
     rehearse the shit out of them until it
     looks like you're hearing it for the
     first time.

MARLA PIERCE, a not particularly attractive woman in
her mid twenties, vacant face, lingers near Luther as
the others move.

                    MARLA

     Stan, I did it last night...

                    SHARON

     Yeah, we're all real pleased that you
     got laid, Marla.

                    LUTHER

     I know Marla, you had some of the bigger
     laughs in that game.

     (Louder to the rest of the troupe)

     Laughs, in case you were wondering, is
     why we're here.

Sharon makes a motion at Marla, like wiping something
off her nose.

                    MARLA

     Fuck you.

                    COLTON

     So soon after last night? Damn, Wonder
     Woman.

                    LUTHER

     Knock it off, let's get it going.

                     GIL

     For crying out Loud, Stan, let's work
     on some new stuff. We can do "Tell me a
     Joke" in our sleep!

                    LUTHER

     Well I hope it's funnier in your sleep,
     'cause when you're awake on stage,
     you suck. Luther's Law: work on your
     strengths so you can cover your weak
     spots. Like you.

                    MIKE

     Play nice, kids.

                    LUTHER

     You don't like it, Stefanik? There's the
     fuckin' door.

Gil lets the remarks roll off his shoulders as he takes
the stage. Sharon and Tiffany glance at Mike, who tries
to avoid eye contact. Tommy jumps up on stage with
Marla.

INT — APARTMENT — MORNING

SIMON FOSTER sits at the foot of his bed talking on the
phone. He is in his thirties, shaggy hair and beard.
His face is kind, but weary.

                    SIMON

     Did you get the car, Janie? (a beat) No,
     older; something big and ugly. (a beat)
     Yeah, something like that. Uh-huh.

He goes to the dresser and takes a wad of money from

the drawer and then reads a piece of paper that is on top of the dresser.

> Older the better. A what? (A beat) Yeah,
> great. Pick me up at noon? Has Thack
> called you yet? (a beat) Is he Okay?
> He's been kind of… you sure? (a beat)
> I'm not saying that, Janie, he's just
> been acting weird lately, that's all.
> Jesus, never mind. Yeah. Bye.

He puts the phone down and hangs his head.

> What a stupid life.

The words EVICTION NOTICE are visible across the top of the paper in his hand. He whistles as he counts out the money.

SIMON

Wow, did I miss last month, too?

He takes a gun out of the drawer and sets it on top of the dresser and rummages. Soon he produces a sheet of paper with some rough sketches of a bank layout.

SIMON

Hey hey hey.

He studies the paper for a few seconds and then folds it up and puts it with the money. He grabs some underwear and socks from the drawer.

He turns toward the bathroom, an ANKH TATTOO is visible on the back of his neck. He heads into the bathroom and the shower starts.

EXT — SIMON'S FRONT DOOR, AFTERNOON

Simon steps out of his apartment and some VOICES catch his attention. He turns and sees MR. PERKINS, the landlord, arguing with MARY a few doors down.

MARY

> Please, Mr. Perkins, I've got kids, just
> give me another week, I don't start my
> new job until Monday and ...

Mary is obviously upset, she holds a small CHILD in her arms, has another CHILD beside her and a bag of groceries at her feet as she faces the burly landlord.

                    PERKINS

          Well, maybe you shoulda thought it
          through better before you had kids and
          ran him off. When you pay the rent, you
          can get back in, until then, shut the
          fuck up. And it better be soon, I'm
          re-renting next week, and your shit is
          going in the trash.

Perkins sneers at them and heads down the hall past
Simon to the stairwell. Simon watches Mary and her two
kids, now sitting on the floor sobbing. Perkins snarls
as he passes.

                    PERKINS

          What are you looking at, Foster? Same
          goes for you, pay your damn rent al-
          ready. These apartment's ain't free.

                    SIMON

          No problem, I was just coming down to
          pay it dickhead.

The mean smile on Perkin's face is replaced by angered
astonishment. Perkins gets right up in Simon's face.

                    PERKINS

          What did you call me?

                    SIMON

          Oh, I'm sorry. That came out wrong.
          Fuckin' asshole.

Perkins takes a swing at Simon, who grabs the arm
coming at him and twists Perkins around and shoves him
against the wall face-first.

                    SIMON

          Not too tough with someone closer to
          your own weight, are you dickhead?

                    PERKINS

          That's it, Foster, I'm calling the cops
          on your ass!

Perkins pushes himself back away from the wall and
knocks Simon against the hand rail at the top of the
stairs. The rail CREAKS loudly. Perkins then turns and
rushes in on Simon.

                         PERKINS

         I'll knock the fuckin' rent right outta
         your ass, Foster.

                          SIMON

         There's an ugly picture.

Simon ducks away easily as Perkins grabs the hand rail
instead. A loud crack is heard as the rail gives way
and Perkins follows it over the side.

                          SIMON

         Shit. That's gonna leave a mark.

Simon rushes over and looks down three flights. Perkins
has landed in front of another apartment. A COUPLE
coming out the door sees the landlord lying there and
looks up at Simon.

                          SIMON

         Mr. Perkins slipped and fell, call 911.

The woman smirks and laughs.

                          WOMAN

         Yeah, right. As soon as we get back from
         the beach.

They then go about their own business. The unconscious
landlord lays on his back bleeding from his ears and
nose.

Simon walks over to Mary and her kids and crouches to
their face level. The kids wear old, worn clothing.

                          SIMON

         You have someplace you can go, Mary?

                          MARY

         I... I have a brother, but he lives in
         Washington.

                          SIMON

         Call your brother, and get the hell out
         of here.

                          MARY

         I can't, Simon. I haven't got any money.
         Blake.

                    SIMON

          Blake's an abusive piece of crap, and
          you're doing alright to be rid of him.

He stands and takes the wad of bills from his pocket
and stuffs them into her hand.

          Here, this should give you a good start.

                    MARY

          I can't take this, it's your money.

                    SIMON

          No it isn't.

He straightens up, looks at her door, sees the NOTICE
pinned to it, KICKS it in. He looks down at the woman's
son.

                    SIMON

          Pretty cool, huh? Just like a "Power
          Ranger."

The little boy just stares at him.

INT — GYPSY WAGON STAGE — LATE AFTERNOON

Tommy and Marla hang the Granma's Ouija Board sign on
the wall at the back of the stage. Luther stands at the
foot of the stage to watch. The other performers set up
seating and put tent cards on tables.

                    LUTHER

          We got new hooks up, so hopefully it
          won't fall again.

                    MIKE

          If some of us had more control over our
          bodies, it wouldn't have fallen at all.

He stares at Marla, who flips him off

                    MIKE

          Sorry, Marla, I'll be the sole holdout
          on that scrumptious offer.

                    TIFFANY

          It's not just him, Stan, she's hit me
          before, too. She can't do physical shit.

                    LUTHER

          Crybabies.

Mike takes Luther aside behind the stage, they pass
Colton, coming back into the room.

                         COLTON

        Oooh, time for "the talk" again?

                         LUTHER

        Shut up, Blanks.

                         COLTON

        Yes sir, Mr. Luther.

He scurries into the theater

                         LUTHER

        Stuff like that happens all the time,
        Mike.

                         MIKE

        Accidents happen, Stan. On stage, she's
        a fuckin' spaz, and she's gonna serious-
        ly hurt someone. We've had this discus-
        sion a hundred times.

                         LUTHER

        Then why are you still whining?

                         MIKE

        Because she sucks and she hurts people.
        Get rid of her.

He cups his hand under imaginary boobs

        These are the only talent she has and
        you know it.

                         LUTHER

        Luther's Law, Stefanik, tits equal tick-
        ets. People will pay to see her, and we
        make money. That's called "business."

                         MIKE

        Really? Well, then where is all this
        money we're making? We've got three wom-
        en with huge tits. Where is all the mon-
        ey, Stan? We never see any of it.

                         LUTHER

        There's a reason for that.

                    MIKE

     Which is?

                    LUTHER

     You'll know when you need to know. When
     we hit it big, we'll all share it, but
     we need to get there first, and that
     takes cash. Who do you think pays all
     our expenses?

                    MIKE

     When are we going to work some new stuff?

                    LUTHER

     As soon as everybody does the old stuff
     right.

Mike just stares at him.

                    LUTHER

     Anything else?

                    MIKE

     Nope.

He walks quickly out the back and slams the door. Gil
appears and opens the door to the prop room.

                    GIL

     Where's Mike going?

                    LUTHER

     Nowhere. Same as you, Gilbert

Gil snorts out a short laugh and starts to get props
out and pile them on the floor.

INT — CERAMICS STUDIO — DAY

Simon traces a path with a pen on the bank plans he has
drawn. JIM FRANKLIN, THACKERY WASHBURN and JANIE GELLER
stand around the table in the small, cramped room filled
with molds and half-done projects. Most of the space is
taken up with a homemade kiln, cluttered shelves and a
large workbench.

Thackery is a tall, thin man with long, stringy hair
and shifty eyes. He seems distracted.

Janie is in her late twenties, fairly attractive, but
wears too much makeup and not enough clothes.

235

Jim is a large, muscular man. His face rarely registers emotion.

                    SIMON

     At this time, there will only be the one
     guard on duty, you take care of him,
     Jim. Thack is here, covering the door-
     ways to the offices, and I cover this end
     with the bag. Janie, you wait right in
     front with the engine running. We are
     going in and out in like, two minutes.
     No muss, no fuss. "Hello, this is a rob-
     bery, blah blah blah, we take as much
     cash as we can in thirty seconds, thank
     you, goodbye." Small bank. Pretty easy.
     Everybody got it?

They all nod. Thack yawns and stretches.

                    THACK

     I'm bored! When do we get to shoot our
     guns?

                    SIMON

     If you're a good boy, maybe for your
     birthday.

                    THACK

     Cool!

Janie snuggles up to Thack, nibbles his ear

                    JANIE

     You can shoot yer gun with me anytime,
     baby.

Thack and Janie kiss and giggle like school kids. Jim
and Simon exchange glances.

                    JIM

     We're set, Sy.

                    SIMON

     Great, now let's take care of payday.
     Janie, pick us up at four thirty?

                    JANIE

     (Overly dramatic)

     Check.

                    THACK

     Ok, daddy.

Thack and Janie break up their embrace and head out,
Jim goes to work on a lump of clay.

Simon wads up the plans and tosses them into the kiln.
He walks quickly out of the studio.

EXT — GYPSY CART, STREET, DAY

Mike crosses the street to THE FOOL'S COURT, a larger
theater directly across the street. A huge sculpted
fool's head adorns the wall, and the name is spelled
out in lighted letters around it.

Mike goes around the side of the building and enters
through a door.

INT — FOOL'S COURT LOBBY — IMMEDIATELY FOLLOWING

Mike enters the atrium from a hallway and sees TARRY
O'DOUL counting money into the register.

                    TARRY

          Stefanik, coming over to the dark side?

Tarry is a large, well-proportioned man in his fifties,
friendly-looking enough, but he has a hard edge to his
smile. He dresses casually, and his muscular carriage
shows through.

                    MIKE

     Hey, Tarry. No, I'm just slumming.

                    TARRY

     Oh, hey now, son, that hurts.

                    MIKE

     Just kidding, man. How'd they do last
     night?

                    TARRY

     Really well, that Businessman one killed
     'em. Sure you don't want to stop this
     cloak and dagger crap and join us?
     You're better'n most my writers.

                    MIKE

     I'm better than all your writers, Tarry,
     and when I come over, I'm bringing Gran-
     ma.

> TARRY
>
> Not as long as Luther's with you, you ain't. "Cocky and talented" I can take. "Asshole" wears me out fast.

> MIKE
>
> I hear you.

Tarry studies Mike for a moment

> TARRY
>
> Go see Terri, she's got a check for both your sketches.

> MIKE
>
> Thanks, man.

Tarry nods and finishes counting as another MAN enters and starts to talk to him.

> MAN
>
> O'Doul, it's about time.

Mike walks down the hall toward the office, passing a doorway through which he catches the rehearsal going on in the main showroom.

On stage, A MAN does a poor job of impersonating President Clinton, and a WOMAN plays a young female intern.

> CLINTON
>
> Hi, and welcome to the oval ORA-fice.

He leers toward the audience

> INTERN
>
> Oh, Mr. President, I'm so honored to be your new intern! I hope it's not too HARD…

She makes an "I'm a BAD little girl" look.

> CLINTON
>
> Well, I won't lie, it's pretty hard!

> INTERN
>
> Oh! Mr. President, you're naughty!

> CLINTON
>
> Darlin', I'd like to get something straight here..

The DIRECTOR stops the action, waving her arms

                    DIRECTOR

          No no no, the line is "I'd like to get
          something STRAIGHT between us," you have
          to say it that way or the call back in
          the "I'm too sexy for my Office" song
          doesn't work. You have to PUNCH it. Try
          it again.

They start to repeat it, Mike watches for a few
moments, shakes his head and glances back down the hall
toward Tarry.

                    MIKE

          Jeez-us, are they still doing that crap?

Tarry and the man have become involved in a heated
argument. Angry sounds are heard, although the exact
words can not be made out.

The man POINTS angrily. Tarry grabs the FINGER in his
fist. He jerks his fist up and gives it a sharp downward
snap. Mike can HEAR the Loud, sickening CRACK.

                    MAN

          What the hell!

The man recoils in agony and doubles over, covering his
hand. Tarry bends a little and whispers into the man's
ear. The man just nods quickly and backs away, then
tuns to leave.

                    TARRY

          And tell that fat bastard I don't talk
          to his flunkies.

Tarry straightens and watches him go. He closes the
till, takes the key out, and then walks away.

Mike just stares and then mouths the word "DAMN."

INT — GYPSY CART STAGE — DAY

Granma's Ouija Board is on stage. Luther addresses the
other members, minus Mike.

                    LUTHER

          Remember, scouts are here tonight. They
          like what they see and we're on our way
          to LA next month for one weekend. Paid.

                    SHARON

     How much paid?

                    LUTHER

     $300. Each.

                    COLTON

     Mother...

                    LUTHER

     And if they like us, we're in for one
     month. Paid. That's eight more shows.

                    TOMMY

     O'Doul know that?

                    LUTHER

     That moron doesn't care, he only cares
     how much he'd have to pay us.

                    GIL

     When are we going to the Big Room, Lu-
     ther?

                    LUTHER

     Soon as I get a better deal.

                    GIL

     We've heard that for months now. And
     just what is he offering?

                    LUTHER

     You want to work for seventy-five a week?

                    SHARON

     It's better'n what we get now.

                    LUTHER

     Bite me.

                    SHARON

     Nah, I don't like finger foods.

                    LUTHER

     Seventy-five ain't shit, we deserve at
     least two hundred. You start at a low
     rate, they'll treat you like shit,
     and make you feel glad to get it, and

they'll have you by the balls for the
rest of your life. After we kill in LA,
he'll offer more.

                    SHARON

Bullshit.

                    LUTHER

You don't like it, Sharon, there's the
fuckin' door.

                    SHARON

Sorry, that's against the "Law."

She pushes her breasts up with her hands

Cause I sell lots of tickets.

Luther turns red with anger.

                    LUTHER

Everybody's replaceable.

                    SHARON

(mocking him) Anything else?

                    LUTHER

Yeah. Somebody go get Stefanik, he's
probably next door crying in his pizza.

He goes to the bar and grabs a beer, pops it and starts
to drink.

                    TIFFANY

I'll get him. I need some air.

                    LUTHER

Gil, you hang around after the show tonight, we're having notes.

                    GIL

Does it have to be tonight? Can't we do
it Monday before rehearsal?

                    LUTHER

I know you can't wait to go change dia-
pers and watch Letterman with the wife,
but we need to meet after the show. I
got shit to do tomorrow.

                              GIL

          Yeah, whatever.

                            LUTHER

          Take five while we wait for Mike and Tif-
          fany.

He picks up a pen and throws himself onto a stool and
starts to scribble notes in his notebook while he
drinks.

INT — FOOL'S COURT HALLWAY — DAY

Mike approaches a door, knocks and enters the office.
Tarry's wife, TERRI O'DOUL sits at the desk with ELLEN,
the office assistant.

                            MIKE

          Excuse me.

                            TERRI

          Oh...

Terri is in her fifties. She is a large, angry,
frustrated woman, who looks as though she is about to
be caught lying or doing something illegal.

                            MIKE

          Hey, Terri. Tarry said you have a check
          ready for me.

She works up a very insincere smile and manner when
she looks up. She quickly hides whatever it is she was
working on.

                            TERRI

          Oh, hi, Mike. Yes, here... the one
          sketch did pretty well. We may use it
          again.

Mike takes the check, looks at it. Looks up at Terri

                            TERRI

          Is there something wrong, Mike?

                            MIKE

          Tarry said he used both last night, and
          they did really well. This is only for
          one of them.

                    TERRI

     Oh. Well, I didn't realize you wrote
     that other one. Can I make it up next
     week? I'm late for rehearsal.

                    MIKE

     I kinda need it this week, if you don't
     mind.

Terri grabs the check out of his hand and tears it up.
She gives up even trying to look pleasant. She turns to
ELLEN, a mousy young woman with a kind face.

                    TERRI

         Ellen, re-write that check, please, and
         void the original. Two sketches.

She gets up and glares at Mike, who is trying to smile
politely, and then storms from the room.

Ellen looks up at Mike.

                    MIKE

     Hey.

                    ELLEN

     Hey.

She proceeds to write the check.

INT — SPIROS' PIZZA — DAY

Tiffany pokes her head in the door and speaks to the
tall, gangly MAN behind the counter who is working some
pizza dough. He speaks with a heavy accent.

                    SPIROS

     Heyo, Tiffany.

                    TIFFANY

     Hi Spiros, have you seen Mike?

                    SPIROS

     Yah, I see him go to Fool about ten min-
     ute past.

                    TIFFANY

     Thanks, Spiros.

She turns to leave, Spiros calls back and stops her

                    SPIROS

     Heyo, Tiffany, you give my name tonight,
     Yah? I give pizza for rehearsal.

                    TIFFANY

     Sure, Spiros, I'll let Stan know.

                    SPIROS

     Thank you, you kids alright.

Tiffany smiles and leaves.

EXT — SPIROS' PIZZA — FOLLOWING

Tiffany sees Mike coming out of the side door to the
Fools' Court. She trots across the street him.

                    TIFFANY

     Mike, we're starting up, you need to get
     back.

                    MIKE

     Yeah, ain't that the sad part.

                    TIFFANY

     What?

                    MIKE

     That I actually need to.

He looks at Tiffany for a second, she doesn't even
mention the CHECK in his hand. He stuffs the check in
his pocket as they cross the street.

                    MIKE

     You heard back from New York?

                    TIFFANY

     No. Not yet. Besides, I think I should
     hang with Granma for another year, get
     more experience. Then

                    MIKE

     Damn it, Tiff. Go to New York. You don't
     get that kind of offer every day. You
     ain't getting shit here. You could stay
     here for another five years and you'd be
     right where you are now. He'll never let
     you get noticed for your talent.

                    TIFFANY

    Well, he's gonna have to learn to, Mike.
    I'm getting it done next week.

                    MIKE

    No shit?

                    TIFFANY

    Yeah, I'm a little scared.

                    MIKE

    You'll be alright. You need anything?
    You got a ride and all that?

                    TIFFANY

    Yeah, I'm okay. Just cover for me, I'll
    be back soon as I can.

                    MIKE

    No problem.

Tiffany gives him a hug, and they head into the back
door of The Gypsy Cart.

EXT — SUBURB STREET — AFTERNOON

Simon, Janie and Jim sit in a car at the curb of an
apartment building. Simon stares at his watch.

                    SIMON

    Where the hell is he?

Janie sits behind the wheel and smokes a cigarette. Jim
stares out the window.

                    SIMON

    He said he'd be ready?

                    JANIE

    Said he'd be ready.

                    SIMON

    It's heading toward five. We have to get
    going, damn it.

                    JANIE

    He'll be out.

Simon looks at his watch for a few more seconds.

                    SIMON

     Screw him, They'll close. Go.

Janie is pissed, but shrugs and starts to pull away.

                    JIM

     Hold on.

They all turn and see Thack come walking out of the
building, smoking, carrying a bag. He takes his time
getting into the car. He leans over and kisses Janie.

                    THACK

     Hey, Bonnie

                    JANIE

     Hey, Clyde.

                    SIMON

     Hey, hey Paula... Come on, man, let's
     get the hell out of here already,
     they're closing up.

She floors it and peels away from the curb.

INT — CAR — FOLLOWING

                    SIMON

     You guys set?

                    JIM

     Yeah.

                    JANIE

     Yes, boss.

                    SIMON

     Thack?

                    THACK

     I can't remember, tell me again?

                    SIMON

     Quit screwing around, man.

                    THACK

     Am I in the drawing room with a candle
     stick?

Janie laughs, Jim almost smiles.

                    SIMON

        Why the hell do you ask for a plan if
        you don't want to use it?

                    THACK

        Oh, come on, Sy, loosen up. You're so
        damn serious and uptight with this shit.

                    SIMON

        Because this is serious work, Thack.
        This ain't nickles and dimes. We screw
        this up, we go away for some real time.

                    JANIE

        Would you two kiss and make up already?

Jim looks sideways at Thack, then back at Simon, who
tries to avoid eye contact.

                    SIMON

          (sighs big) I just don't want to blow
          it, that's all.

Thack turns for a moment, serious.

                    THACK

        Nobody does, man. Chill.

He turns back. Janie quickly glances at Simon in the
rear-view mirror.

INT — GYPSY CART STAGE — DAY

Everyone except for Luther is onstage facing the seats.
Luther sits in the audience facing the stage, empty
beer bottles lie at his feet. Gil is front and center
on stage.

                    GIL

        OK, We need a kind of person...

                    LUTHER

        A nigger!

Gil shakes his head in embarrassment. Stan laughs
hysterically.

                    COLTON

        Wow. Nice one, there, Jew Boy.

Luther points a finger at Colton.

                    Luther

Hey now, that's racist.

                    GIL

Okay, okay. The first thing I heard was
a "Rigger," who, as we all know, is a
person who rigs sailing ships.

                  LUTHER

No, I said NIGGER.

He laughs Loudly. Tiffany jumps downstage, beating Mike
and Marla to the punch.

                  TIFFANY

So, anyway, a Nun, a Commie and a Rigger are walking down the street when the
Rigger suddenly runs into a store. The
Nun and the commie wait for what seems
like hours, then the Rigger comes out
with his arms full of bags. The nun and
the commie ask, "What took you so long,
and why did you buy all that crap?!" The
Rigger says "You know me, I always get
caught up in a SALE!"

Everybody claps and whoops. Mike leaps forward

                  MIKE

A nun, a commie and a rigger are walking
down the street. The nun asks the rigger
if he went to school for that. He says
"no, I went to school to play football."
The Commie says, "Oh, what did you do on
the team?" And the rigger says "block
and tackle…"

More clapping and cheers. He steps back and Marla runs
in to take his place.

                  MARLA

A nun, a commie and a rigger are walking
down the street. The Commie asks what
the rigger's favorite song is, and he
says "Eleanor Rigby."

This gets lots of odd looks from the cast, some polite
applause. Tommy jumps forward.

                    TOMMY

          OK! A nun, a commie, and "Astro" from
          "the Jetsons" are walking down the
          street in Alabama...

Everybody boos him and drags him back into line where
they pretend to beat the shit out of him. Luther laughs
his ass off, then waves his arms.

                    LUTHER

          That's enough. Let's get something
          to eat.

EXT — LA CITY STREET — AFTERNOON

Thackery Gang car pulls up to the curb in front of a
bank. Thack is jittery.

                    THACK

          Start the clock, Simon. Let's go.
          Let's go.

Jim, Simon and Thack get out and glance around, they
wear rolled-up ski masks on their heads. Simon checks
his watch and looks up.

                    SIMON

     Now.

Thack, Jim and Simon look up and down the street, then
quickly roll the masks down to cover their faces as
they enter the bank.

INT — BANK LOBBY — FOLLOWING

There are about a dozen people in the lobby. The doors
to two offices are open, and the rooms are empty.

An older SECURITY GUARD flips through some bank
literature at a display, and does not take notice as
they enter. Simon makes his move.

                    SIMON

          Alright, people...

Thack suddenly fires his automatic pistol at the
security camera, destroying it.

                    SIMON

          (to himself) What are you doing?

                         THACK

          Listen up, people! Keep your hands off
          the alarm buttons.

There is a general state of fear and confusion as
people realize what is happening. Most customers DROP
to the floor and cower.

Thack FIRES wildly at the walls breaking fixtures and
sending debris flying until his gun clicks empty.

                         THACK

          What the?

The security guard near Thack hears the clicking of the
weapon and goes for his own GUN. Jim pulls a SHOTGUN
from under his coat and levels it at him.

                          JIM

          Nope. Put 'em up, Barney.

Jim keeps the rifle steady with one hand as he reaches
and takes the guard's gun with the other.

People watch as Thack searches his coat for his extra
ammo, but can't find it. He lowers his gun and shouts to
be heard.

                         THACK

          We picked your bank because there's al-
          ways six openings at the counter, but
          only two tellers at any given time. That
          pisses me off. You also never have pens
          in your tubes at the drive through. Like
          how fucking hard is it to put pens in
          there as common courtesy? And exact-
          ly who is the freaking rocket scientist
          that came up with charging you to write
          checks for your own fucking money? But
          first, I have a little transaction to
          take care of.

He glances over to Simon who stands looking wide eyed
at Thack, then finally heads for the counter, pulling
a plastic bag out of his jacket and tossing it to the
TELLER.

                         SIMON

          Fill it. Leave the rigged shit and
          change. Gimmee them deposit bags, too.

250

The tellers do as he says. One looks up at Thack, he aims his empty gun at her, she makes a face.

                              THACK

          Keep them eyes on your work, I'd hate
          for you to make a mistake counting it
          out and then come up short at the end of
          the day.

Simon looks down at his watch.

                              SIMON

          Thirty seconds, man.

The tellers finish throwing money in the bag, Simon takes it back.

                              THACK

          DING! Thank you very much.

A movement catches Thack's attention. A WOMAN comes out of a bathroom in the hallway. Thack turns and pulls the trigger out of nervousness. The gun clicks.

                              THACK

          Shit. Get over there. On the floor.

Thack scans the faces in the lobby and bites his lip. The woman does as he said.

Simon takes the bag and knots the opening, then throws it to Jim. The three back toward the door.

                              SIMON

          Let's rock, man.

Thack races to the counter and leans in really close to the tellers.

                              THACK

          Is there going to be some sort of... uh,
          non-instant cash, ATM terminal bullshit
          fee for this withdrawal?

The tellers don't know how to react, they stare. Finally one almost whispers.

                              TELLER

          N... no...

                              Luther

          Yee-haw! I love this bank.

He tries to rip a COUNTER PEN off its chain, it takes a few tries. He whirls and runs out.

INT — THE GYPSY CART — EVENING

People fill the seats in front of the stage, they are drinking, having a great time. LIGHTS play on the stage. The background MUSIC fades out and the spot on the stage dims as we hear Tommy on the mic.

> TOMMY VO
>
> Good evening Ladies and Gentlemen, and welcome to The Gypsy Cart. Before we start the show, here is a word from one of our sponsors.

> COLTON VO
>
> Tonight's show is brought to you by Spiros' Pizza, about a block down the street. Spiros' Pizza... he gives us free food!

> TOMMY VO
>
> And now, Do you know what the future holds in store for you? (a beat) well, neither do we! But please welcome the troupe who will make it fun to not know what's coming next, GRANMA'S OUIJA BOARD!

The troupe rushes onstage as their THEME MUSIC is played by the keyboardist. They goof with their own personal poses or gestures. As the applause and music die down Mike steps front and center, with the rest of the troupe milling about behind him.

> MIKE
>
> Alright, good crowd, good crowd! Except for that rat bastard back there by the bar, Chelsea, throw that guy out.

CHELSEA, the bartender, blows the duck whistle she has on a chain around her neck, the audience laughs.

> MIKE
>
> Just kidding, let that rat bastard stay, we get a take of the bar. You guys ready for some Improv?

The audience roars in the affirmative.

                    MIKE

        Well then let's rip. As you all may
        know, in improv, we make up stuff as we
        go along, with a little help from our
        close, personal friends, YOU. For
        instance, if I were to ask you for a
        color...

He points exaggeratedly toward the room, an AUDIENCE
MEMBER yells

                    PERSON

        Green.

The troupe claps and cheers, joined by the audience.

                    MIKE

        That's right, it's just that easy! And
        if we were to ask for a geographical lo-
        cation, we'd get...

Again he points, someone yells.

                    PERSON

        Omaha!

Again the troupe claps and cheers.

                    MIKE

        Oh, you poor, poor, lonely man. But yes,
        that would be correct! And, if we were
        to ask for your phone number...

He points right at a cute woman in the front row, she
is a little embarrassed.

                    WOMAN

        No way, loser.

                    MIKE

        Ouch, that hurts just as much no
        matter how often you hear it. But to
        get on with it, let's start with a
        cute little game that requires an
        audience volunteer.

He plays with the audience a bit and doesn't notice
Tarry O'Doul at the back of the room leaning against a
pillar. Tarry shakes his head and smiles.

Mike helps a woman up onto the stage.

                    MIKE

     Thank you so much. What's your name?

                    WOMAN

     Barbara Noonan.

                    MIKE

     Let's have a big round of applause for
     Barbara Noonan, giving it up for the
     team! Thank you so much, Barbara. And
     now, we are going to play a silly lit-
     tle game that we like to call "You Lying
     Sack of Shit!" Here's how it works. Me
     and Sharon...

He yanks Sharon out of line as the rest of the cast
exits the stage and takes up positions off to side.

                    MIKE

     ...are police investigators, and we are
     investigating a huge, unsolved crime —
     AUDIENCE!

The audience starts to shout out crimes such as The
TITANIC sinking, LINDBERGH baby kidnapping etc. We hear
BOB CRANE'S murder a little louder than the rest

                    MIKE

     The huge crime of the century, the
     Murder of Actor Bob Crane

He does a quick take to the audience.

     Who is the sick freak who gave us that?
     Cut off table six.

Chelsea blows the duck whistle. Tarry laughs.

                    SHARON

     Here's how it works, "Barbara" we can
     link you to the murder of Bob Crane,
     we know you did it, and anything you
     say can prove it! What do you do for a
     living, "Barbara?"

                    BARBARA

     I'm a consultant with Langdon and
     Arbuckle.

                    MIKE/SHARON

You Lying Sack Of Shit!

                      SHARON

Ha, I knew it! That was a big mistake,
missy! You're going up the river now.
Consultant, Huh? You mean like answering
questions?

Sharon and Mike circle Barbara slowly and make gestures
at her as they speak.

                        MIKE

Like questioning authority?

                      SHARON

Which is just like the 64 thousand
dollar question?

                        MIKE

Which takes us to a thousand points of
light, am I right?

                      SHARON

And then George Bush...

                        MIKE

Who was with the CIA...

                      SHARON

A counterpart to the KGB...

                        MIKE

And the Gestapo.

                      SHARON

In World War two.

                        MIKE

Prisoner of War camps.

                      SHARON

Gulags and Stalags.

                        MIKE

Stalag 13.

                      SHARON

Hogan's Heroes.

                        BOTH

              YOU KILLED BOB CRANE!

The audience loves it. They menace Barbara who is ready
to pee her pants from laughing.

                       TARRY

          Jeez, he's wastin' it over here.

He looks down at his watch and quickly crosses to the
bar. He writes something on a napkin and hands it to
Chelsea. He leans in to be heard over the din.

                       TARRY

          Give that to Mike when he's done,
          please.

                      CHELSEA

          No problem, Tarry.

                       TARRY

          And tell him it's "MISTER Rat Bastard."

She laughs and Tarry grins as he hurries out the back
of the room.

Luther, just off stage, notices Tarry leaving. He goes
to the bar.

                      LUTHER

          What did he want?

                      CHELSEA

          He just said to give this to Mike.

She shows the note, Luther grabs it.

                      LUTHER

          I'll give it to him.

He reads it, shakes his head, makes a face toward the
door, then wads it up and tosses it in the trash.

                      BARBARA

          No, I didn't do it!

                    MIKE/SHARON

          You Lying Sack Of Shit!

                      SHARON

          And just to show that it wasn't a fluke,

we can do it backwards, too.

                    MIKE

That's right, Barbara, you did kill Bob
Crane.

                    SHARON

Who played Colonel Hogan.

                    MIKE

And ate Colonel Sanders.

                    SHARON

Not really the colonel, but his fried
chicken.

                    MIKE

Formerly Chicken Little.

                    SHARON

And the Little Red Hen.

                    MIKE

Who said "the sky is falling."

                    SHARON

Planets and stars.

                    MIKE

A star is born.

                    SHARON

Crappy movie remake with BARBARA Strei-
sand.

                    MIKE

Barbara...

                    SHARON

Noonan...

                    BOTH

You killed Bob Crane!

The audience goes wild as Mike and Sharon have two
"Deputies" drag Barbara off to the bar for a free drink.

EXT — LA CITY FREEWAY — EVENING

The Thackery gang car races down the freeway, we hear
Janie and Thack singing.

                    THACK/JANIE

    Come on, take the money and run.

                         JIM

    OOOH-yeah!

                    THACK/JANIE

    Go on, take the money and run...

                        JANIE

    Come on, Sy, sing along.

                        THACK

    Aw, we hurt his feelings cause we didn't
    stick to his plan.

                        SIMON

    Flying by the seat of your pants is
    one thing, Thack; being totally reck-
    less is another. The fuck is your
    problem lately?

                        THACK

    Hold it steady, baby.

He pulls a gun, turns, and shoves the gun in Simon's
face.

                        JANIE

    What are you doing, Thack?!

                         JIM

    Shit.

                        THACK

    The only thing's gonna be reckless is my
    blowing your head off, Foster. I am in
    charge. You read me?

There is a long a beat.

                        SIMON

    Yeah. You're a regular Al Haig.

Thack glares at Simon for a second or two, then pulls
back the gun and laughs loud.

                        THACK

    Now that is why I like you, man, you say
    some funny shit. Al Haig!

Thack laughs and turns back around. Janie takes a look at Simon in the mirror, their eyes meet briefly. She looks back to Thack and smiles.

Jim looks over at Simon, then leans over.

> JIM
>
> You okay, bro?

> SIMON
>
> As okay as I'm gonna be after shitting my pants.

Jim shakes his head, smiles and leans back, looking out the window.

> THACK
>
> Turn right up here, Janie, we gotta ditch this ride.

The car turns down a dirt road.

INT — GYPSY CART — NIGHT

The troupe is in the middle of another game. Colton, Tiffany, Gil, Luther and Tommy are on stage. Tommy, wearing a black cape, is laughing maniacally with his fists in the air, Luther plays his henchman. Marla "flies" in from off stage and strikes a heroic pose.

> MARLA
>
> Not so fast Professor Cyclops! Back off, before things get ugly.

> TOMMY
>
> (indicating Marla) Too late!

> MARLA
>
> Why you creep, hi-ya!

She goes on a ninja-esque killing spree, knocking down Tiffany and Gil, then knees Tommy in the groin. He doubles over in real pain.

> COLTON
>
> She's killed Professor Cyclops!

> LUTHER
>
> Aww, nuts.

Tommy staggers off the side of the stage like a ruptured duck holding his package. The audience laughs and claps, the lights go out. After a few seconds of darkened applause, the stage lights come back up and we here Colton on the mic.

                    COLTON VO

          Our regular announcer is a little "test-
          ee" tonight, so I'll be replacing him.

Laughs and groans from the audience.

EXT — JIM'S HOUSE/STUDIO — NIGHT

A beat up car pulls into an old one-car shed. Jim and Simon get out. Jim opens the trunk and takes out his bag. They head in the side door to the house.

INT — LIVING ROOM — IMMEDIATELY FOLLOWING

Jim throws his bag on the floor, heads to the kitchen. On the way he points to a couch.

                    JIM

          You know where your bed is, man.

                    SIMON

          Thanks for letting me hang here for a
          while, Jim.

                    JIM

          No problem, Sy. We better go pick up
          your shit like, tomorrow or something,
          huh? Beer?

He opens the fridge and rummages in it.

Simon sits on the couch's armrest, picks up a small ceramic object, not really looking at it.

                    SIMON

          Nah. Nothing there I need. That friggin'
          landlord is gonna have me shot when he
          gets out of the hospital.

                    JIM

          Maybe he'll die.

                    SIMON

          Jesus, thanks, Jimbo, I feel better
          already.

Jim comes into the room with a six pack and tosses one to Simon, then pops one for himself.

                    JIM

Solve your problem, though, can't talk
if he's dead.

                    SIMON

Yeah, but then I'm a murderer.

                    JIM

So who's gonna know? Sounds like he
started it, anyway.

                    SIMON

Yeah, guess so.

Jim sits down heavily on a big wooden crate, sets his
beer on the floor, and takes off his outer shirt. Then he
picks up his beer again, kills it, grabs another.

                    JIM

I knew Thackery since we was kids. We'd
steal little shit here and there. Got
busted twice before we was teenagers.
His parents sent him off to college hop-
ing to turn him around. He dropped out a
year later.

                    SIMON

Yeah. He was still pulling the same old
crap when I met him. Used to be kinda
fun. But I'm sick of this now. I want to
get out.

                    JIM

I figured as much.

                    SIMON

Yeah?

                    JIM

Thack know?

                    SIMON

Shit. Thack care?

                    JIM

Starting to look like a big fat "no" on
that one, bro.

                         SIMON

          What is his deal, Jimbo?

Jim shakes his head slowly and pops his third beer

                           JIM

          Hell if I know. He's been acting weird
          lately. We been doing mostly small jobs
          with no problem. But since we been hit-
          ting bigger and bigger, it's like he's
          getting a swelled head, like one of them
          rock stars that smashes hotel rooms.

                         SIMON

          Think he'll be okay for next month?

                           JIM

          Damn well better be, Homes.

Jim gets up and downs the beer. He goes and locks the
door and heads into the other room.

                           JIM

          See you in the morning, man.

                         SIMON

          Later.

          Jim stops in the kitchen and turns back.

                           JIM

          What you want to do then?

                         SIMON

          (almost laughing) Something different.

                           JIM

          Yeah. Completely different.

He leaves. Simon finishes his beer and looks at the
object in his hand. It is woman's head, beautiful, sad.
Simon sees Jim's name on it.

                         SIMON

          Wow.

He puts the piece down where he got it from, turns out
the light and lays down on the couch.

INT — GYPSY CART STAGE — AFTERNOON

Everyone except Tiffany is present. Luther is sitting at
the bar writing in his notebook.

> LUTHER

Hey, Mike, when is Tiffany coming back?

> MIKE

She'll be back for Friday's show, I
talked to her yesterday.

> LUTHER

Why didn't she call me?

> MIKE

She did, your phone is disconnected.

> LUTHER

Oh.

> GIL

How is LA shaping up, Stan?

> TOMMY

Oh, yeah, are we flying in, driving,
what?

> LUTHER

We're renting a van and driving. And I
don't know about the rest of you, but I
plan on being in the air about two hours
outside of town.

> MARLA

Ooh, a little of the wacky weed, the
smoke on a rope, mary-wanna. I'm riding
with you.

Sharon, Gil and Mike all sit close together. Mike
speaks just loud enough for them to hear.

> MIKE

Why doesn't she just puff on his cigar
and get it over with.

Gil and Sharon smirk and stifle laughs.

> LUTHER

I'm getting magnetic signs made for the
van so we can get some advertising on
the trip. Two rooms at the Sleep-n-Leave

> for Friday night, and we'll drive back
> on Saturday after the show.

                    GIL

Isn't that kind of pushing it?

                    LUTHER

No.

                    TOMMY

Are we gonna use any new sketches or
games?

                    LUTHER

No, for this gig we better just use
the ones we know work. We'll pull out
the new stuff when they book us for the
month.

                    SHARON

Ooh, takin' chances, pushin' the enve-
lope.

                    GIL

Smokin' the rope.

They laugh, Marla even laughs a little. Luther is
annoyed, but sarcastically joins in

                    LUTHER

Kissing my ass, pussy-whipped and goin'
bald. I gotta go leave a message for
Chelsea.

He gets up and grabs a beer out of the bar and stalks
out. Tommy and Marla chat excitedly. Gil sits at a
table next to and Sharon and Mike.

                    SHARON

How can you take so much shit from him,
Gil? Doesn't he drive you nuts?

                    MIKE

No kidding.

                    GIL

First of all, I don't give two shits
about Stan Luther. He's nothing to me.
I'm married, I got kids, I have a life.

He does that to make himself feel
better. I do my shows and go home.

                SHARON

So go to another troupe, you can't swing
a dead musician without hitting another
improv troupe in this town.

                 GIL

Nah. We started Granma, and it's made
a name for itself. I'll stick with it
until it's gone.

                MIKE

I know what you mean.

                 GIL

Yeah. Which brings up a second point.
Why do you take so much shit from him
lately, Mike? Aren't you supposed to be
one of the co-owners or something?

                SHARON

What's going on with you these days. You
walk around like that guys whackin' you
with a rolled up newspaper every night.

                MIKE

I don't know, man. He's such a bastard,
you know. He slowly but surely made it
so that everything is in his name now.
On paper, he owns it, but we do all the
work.

                SHARON

So let's all leave.

                MIKE

Well, it's kinda like Gil said. We
started this troupe from nothing. Name
recognition goes a long way. It'd be
hard to start over.

                 GIL

BS, man. The name don't mean shit. If he
re-stocks the tank with new people and
they suck — let's say, a tank full of
Marlas and Tommies —

They all look toward Tommy and Marla, who are deeply engulfed in a mutual admiration chat.

> TOMMY
>
> Oh, that was so funny last night when you did that scene for the movie review.

> MARLA
>
> Are you kidding? You playing Marlon Brando as Richard Simmons ruled.

> TOMMY
>
> I don't know where I got that from.

They turn back to their conversation

> GIL
>
> ...he's got nothing. Let's do it. After LA. We say "Now performing, uh, Granpa's Cribbage Board" starring so-and-so, formerly of blah blah blah." The people'll know the score, and in no time we're on top again. And we blow his white, pock-marked, hairy ass out of the water.

Mike and Sharon just stare at him.

> SHARON
>
> I thought you didn't care.

> GIL
>
> Aw, I'm a big fuckin' liar, man.

Luther comes back into the room.

> LUTHER
>
> Okay, Let's work on the sketches for tonight. Marla, fill in for Tiffany's part for The Hunchback.

They all converge on the stage.

EXT — LA CITY SIDE STREET — DAY

Thack talks on a pay phone for a few moments, we can not hear what is being said. He nods a couple of times.

> THACK
>
> Thanks, man.

He hangs up, walks quickly to the waiting car at the
curb and gets in. Janie sits behind the wheel smoking.

                    JANIE

Well, what did they say?

                    THACK

It's on.

                    JANIE

Where do we meet them?

                    THACK

I left it open. Told them I'd call them
after the job. They'll take care of the
cash for us, and get us out of the country. Then we're home free, baby!

                    JANIE

This is so exciting! Simon and Jim are
gonna bust a vein.

                    THACK

To hell with them, baby. This one is for
us. I'm cutting them both loose. They'll
still get a share, but they're on their
own.

                    JANIE

Why?

                    THACK

I'm getting sick of Sy's shit, and I
ain't getting' caught cause of his ass.

                    JANIE

What about Jim?

                    THACK

Huh, he wants out anyway. I can tell.
His heart ain't in it no more. We need
people on the edge, like us.

                    JANIE

Yeah, I guess so.

                    THACK

Let's go.

The car pulls away from the curb and drives off.

EXT — LA CITY STREET — DAY

Jim and Simon sit in a car across the street from a jewelry store. It is a relatively small, not very busy looking shop, with a long alley down the side of it that goes all the way to the next cross street.

> JIM VO
>
> Not much to look at. They got that kind of money?

> SIMON VO
>
> It's not just them, Jimbo. They're the last stop on a run that includes five banks and three other jewelry stores.

He looks at his watch.

> Check this out. In about ten seconds the truck pulls in at the other end of the alley.

An armored truck pulls into the alley at the far side. It comes through and pulls out into the street Simon and Jim are on, and parks in front of the store. Two guards get out.

> SIMON
>
> Same exact time every day.

> JIM
>
> Them ain't rent-a-cops, Sy, they for real strapped. And it's right in the middle of the street.

> SIMON
>
> We're not going to hit them in the street. Come on, let's go, I'll tell you on the way back.

> JIM
>
> Yo.

Jim starts the car and it pulls away from the curb and drives away.

> JIM
>
> Hey, you read the paper today?

                    SIMON

     What's up?

                    JIM

     Your luck is holding out, man. Landlord
     died last night. Cops are calling it an
     accident.

                    SIMON

     No shit?

                    JIM

     Yeah, when they investigated at the
     apartments, the railing fell apart in
     their hands. They figured he fell.
     Nobody saw anything. Everybody hated
     him. Ironic justice. Case closed.

                    SIMON

     Wow.

                    JIM

     Yeah.

Simon stares out the window as the car speeds away.

INT — GYPSY CART STAGE — DAY

Luther faces the troupe, which is on stage.

                    LUTHER

     Stop upstaging each other. If you're
     doing a cross, come on, do it, and get
     the hell off. You're taking away from the
     main action if you stay any longer.

                    COLTON

     What about last week when you came on as
     the goat and stayed the whole damn time?

This is met with "yeah's" and "what about that's"

                    LUTHER

     Oh, come on, livestock is always funny,
     especially with Tommy.

Two police OFFICERS enter at back of the theater. They
walk up a little way into the room.

                    OFFICER 1

     Excuse me.

                    SHARON

          Wanna play, Stan?

Luther stares death at Sharon, then turns and addresses
the officers.

                    LUTHER

          Can I help you?

                    OFFICER 2

          We hope so. We're looking for someone
          who used to work here. Marvin Peters.
          Anyone know him?

Sharon steps down from the stage and stands near
Luther.

                    SHARON

          Marvin Peters? Hmmm, Sounds really fa-
          miliar. You know him, don't you, Stan?

                    LUTHER

          No, but he used to work here a few years
          ago. No one's heard from him in a long
          time. Why?

                    OFFICER 1

          Police business.

                    SHARON

          Should we be afraid of him? I mean, has
          he killed anyone?

                    OFFICER 1

          No. Checks mostly. That kind of thing.

Sharon nods quickly in agreement and adds

                    SHARON

          Ah, real asshole type, huh? Restraining
          orders, that kind of stuff?

The cop smiles. He approaches Sharon and Luther,
handing them CARDS.

                    OFFICER 1

          Yeah, sort of. If any of you hear from
          him, please give us a call.

SHARON

No problem.

OFFICER 2

Thank you. Have a good one.

LUTHER

Yeah. You too.

The officers leave. Luther turns to Sharon

LUTHER

Have fun?

SHARON

Yeah. You? (she smacks her forehead)
Damn! Forgot to get them free passes.
Ooh, I have his card.

Luther shoots her an angry look, then turns back to
continue with the cast on stage.

INT — JIM'S STUDIO — AFTERNOON

Thack, Janie, Jim and Simon stand around the workbench
as Simon points down to a big piece of paper and
explains.

SIMON

When we stop the truck here, it has got
to go fast. We can't give the guards a
chance to gather their wits, or we're
dead. We can knock them out, empty the
truck and be gone in under two minutes.
This is it, the big one. Should be about
half a million.

THACK

How the hell do you know?

SIMON

Cause, Thack, I didn't just wake up one
day and say "let's go knock over an armored truck." I followed the truck a few
times, I've seen what they haul. I do
homework, I plan. I ain't stupid.

THACK

Okay, okay, whatever. I'm not stupid,
either.

                    JANIE

        He didn't say you were, baby.

                    THACK

        Yeah, well, I'm not.

They all stare at each other in silence for a few
seconds.

                    SIMON

        Okay. Here's how it goes down. Exactly.

He starts to explain the plan.

EXT — SPIROS' PIZZA GARDEN COURTYARD — DAY

Granma's Ouija Board, minus Tiffany hang out, drink
beer and margaritas. Tommy smokes a huge cigar. Luther
drinks from his own huge quart beer bottle.

                    LUTHER

        The photographer will be here in like
        five minutes. Where's Tiffany?

                    MIKE

        She's on her way. She called Sharon as
        she was leaving.

                    LUTHER

        Well she better get here soon, we need
        these new publicity shots to take to LA.

                    COLTON

        What's wrong with our old shots?

                    LUTHER

        She ain't in them.

                    COLTON

        A couple of us aren't in them. That
        hasn't seemed to bother you before. Ar-
        en't we cute enough to warrant new pics?

Luther ignores him and continues writing in his book.

                    COLTON

        Dick.

The door leading into the courtyard from Spiros' opens
and Tiffany appears, wearing a T-shirt. We immediately
notice her obvious decrease in chest size.

                    MIKE

     Hey, Tiff. Glad to have you back.

                   SHARON

     God DAMN, girlfriend!

Luther looks up and does a DOUBLE-TAKE. He shakes his
head only slightly and keeps writing. The rest of the
troupe gathers around Tiffany.

                   COLTON

     Thanks for letting us know.

                  TIFFANY

     What, do you own a share in my tits?

                   COLTON

     Well, I was hoping that someday...

                   SHARON

     Shut up, Blanks. You look good, sister.
     Why didn't you say something?

                  TIFFANY

     Because I'm tired of them being more
     interesting than I am.

She notices everybody staring at her chest. There is an
awkward silence, the gawkers suddenly shake themselves
out of their stupor and back off.

              COLTON/TOMMY/GIL

     Sorry.

                   MARLA

     Way to go, Tiff.

She walks away smiling to herself.

                   SHARON

        Come on Tiff, photographer's gonna be
        here soon.

They walk over to where Luther sits. Luther chugs his
huge beer down and looks up.

                   LUTHER

        About time, Carson. Would you two leave
        us alone for a minute?

He looks at Sharon and Mike. They see that look on his face and refuse to budge.

                    SHARON

     Why?

                    LUTHER

     Do I need a reason?

                    MIKE

     Yes.

                    LUTHER

     Can't you both just be courteous and
     back the fuck off?

                    TIFFANY

     What is it, Stan?

She puts her hands on her hips and makes sure her breasts are in plain view of Luther. He really has to work hard not to look at them.

                    LUTHER

     I just need to talk to you for a minute,
     alone.

                    SHARON

     Give me a break, Stan.

                    TIFFANY

     What is it?

                    LUTHER

     (to Sharon and Mike) Back off.

                    MIKE

     Go ahead and say it, Stan, we're all
     friends.

                    LUTHER

     Shut the fuck up, Stefanik.

Sharon, Mike and Luther all start to argue Loudly at the same time. The rest of the troupe sits a few seats away and stares silently.

Tiffany shouts to be heard.

                    TIFFANY

     Just fucking tell me, Stan.

LUTHER

(LOUD) I'm letting you go.

Suddenly it gets real quiet.

TIFFANY

What?

LUTHER

You heard me. You're out. (a beat) I'll
bet you wished I could have told you
quietly now, huh?

There is a collective gasp from the troupe.

SHARON

What about LA? It's next week.

LUTHER

She should have thought about that
before she took off and missed all the
rehearsals.

COLTON

You fucking prick, Luther.

TIFFANY

So that's it?

LUTHER

Like I said. You took two weeks off without letting me know, you haven't been
getting any laughs lately, you show up
late for rehearsals. Want me to go on?

TOMMY

Jesus Christ, Stan, I haven't been
on time to a single rehearsal in two
months.

COLTON

And he sucks

TOMMY

Yeah. And I suck. Like big time.

Luther ignores them and continues his writing. He won't
make eye contact with Tiffany.

                    MIKE

          Luther...

                  TIFFANY

          Let it go, Mike. You are one sad
          mother fucker, Stan. No family, no
          friends...

                  LUTHER

          Stop, I'm gonna cry.

                  TIFFANY

          Go to Hell. Suck my dick, and then go to
          Hell.

She turns and walks away, Sharon catches up with her
and they talk by the door.

Mike stands and stares down at Luther, who ignores him
as long as he can. Finally he looks up.

                  LUTHER

          Anything else, crybaby?

Mike opens his mouth and is about to cut loose, Luther
interrupts quickly.

                  LUTHER

          I mean, anything else before we discuss
          the plans for LA?

He now is clearly addressing the whole troupe.

                  LUTHER

          LA next weekend. Big show. Paid. Produc-
          ers, casting people, studio executives.
          L A? I mean, this is what we've all
          been looking forward to, right?

They are all silent. Luther laughs.

                  LUTHER

          I thought so.

The PHOTOGRAPHER opens the door and almost hits Sharon
and Tiffany. He scoots around them and brings his bags
over to Luther's table.

                PHOTOGRAPHER

          Sorry I'm late.

                    LUTHER

     No problem, Steven. Set up over by the
     fountain.

                  PHOTOGRAPHER

     Alright, how many?

Luther glances at the troupe

                    LUTHER

     Seven.

The photographer nods and starts to set his lights.

EXT — LA CITY STREET — AFTERNOON

An old clunker pulls up to the jewelry store, then
backs into the alley. Thack, Jim and Simon get out.
Janie pops the hood and gets out. Simon takes up his
position at the alley opening.

                    SIMON

     Get moving, Janie.

Thack nods to Jim and the large man opens the trunk of
the car and takes out the JACK and a TOOLBOX. Janie
puts the hood up.

                    JANIE

     See you boys in a few minutes.

She takes another set of keys out of her pocket and
heads back out into the street.

                    THACK

     Careful, Bonnie.

Simon glances toward the car and sees Jim has the front
end raised on the jack. He looks at his watch.

                    SIMON

     Any time now. Be careful, Jimbo.

                     JIM

     You know it, Sy.

Thack steals a glance up the alley and then heads over
to a big dumpster nearby.

               Jim leans over into the car and starts
               to tinker with the engine. He leans back
               out and motions to Simon.

                         JIM

         All set, man. It's showtime.

Simon takes Jim's place under the hood as Jim gets back
into the car in the back seat. He gets down low and
pulls a blanket over himself.

Simon keeps glancing up the alley as he mucks about
under the hood.

                        SIMON

         Come on, baby.

Soon the armored truck pulls into the alley and heads
right for them.

EXT — SPIROS' PIZZA COURTYARD — EVENING

Mike, Gil and Sharon sit at a table and finish off a
pitcher of beer.

                        MIKE

         That's it. This ain't worth it.

                         GIL

         Come on, Mike.

                        MIKE

         Fuck this. I am so sick of him playing
         with people. Who the fuck does he think
         he is?

                       SHARON

         We all know what he's like, and we put
         up with it because he knows how to sell
         us. I don't like him either, but we
         wouldn't have gotten half this far with-
         out him lying, cheating and stealing to
         get us there. If you can't handle that,
         then you're in the wrong business.

                         GIL

         We'll all miss Tiff, Mike, but in a
         warped kind of way, Sharon's right.
         You're a performer, not a businessman.
         You need someone like Luther to get you
         where you're going.

                        MIKE

         Like Luther?

                    GIL

Yeah.

                   MIKE

Bull, they ain't all like him.

                  SHARON

Think about it, Mike. At your level of
the food chain, how are you gonna get
anywhere with a nice guy selling you.

Mike opens his mouth to speak, Sharon cuts him off

        And before you say it, Tarry O'Doul is
        just as bad as the rest of them. That
        guy has ties to organized crime up the
        wazoo.

                    GIL

His ties are so long, they run up my
wazoo.

                  SHARON

No shit, Mike. He's a regular Goodfella.

                   MIKE

How would you know?

                  SHARON

It's true. Stan Luther used to be three
other people, including Marvin Peters.
O'Doul wouldn't help him get a new life
because of his winning personality.
That's why Stan hates him.

                    GIL

How do you know so much, Sharon?

                  SHARON

I used to date Marvin Peters.

                 MIKE/GIL

Holy shit.

                  SHARON

So now you know my dirty little secret.
Anyway, Mike, they're all the same.

                    MIKE

     Yeah, maybe they are, but you don't
     have to go out of your way to screw with
     people.

                    SHARON

     No, You don't. You're right. But don't
     worry about Tiffany, Mike.

                    MIKE

Why?

                    SHARON

     Because she can take care of herself.
     She doesn't NEED this bullshit... she
     just likes doing it.

                    GIL

     Do what you have to, Mike, but keep your
     eyes open. You want to split, I'm with
     you, and I think that with the exception
     of Marla, everyone else is too. I just
     think it's time you stop whining and
     start doing what you're good at.

                    MIKE

Which is?

                    GIL

     Paying for this beer, for one thing.
     Sandy's picking me up in like two min-
     utes out front, I gotta go.

                    SHARON

     Later, Gil.

                    MIKE

     Take it easy.

Gil gets up and leaves. Mike and Sharon are left
staring at each other.

Mike CHINS-UP Sharon, she returns the gesture.

The WAITPERSON comes over to their table and starts to
clear it off.

EXT — JEWELRY STORE ALLEYWAY — LATE AFTERNOON

The armored truck stops near the dumpster. One GUARD

gets out and looks toward Simon and the car, his hand
on his holster.

                              GUARD

          Car trouble?

Simon doesn't look up from under the hood

                              SIMON

          (Loud, sarcastic) Duh.

                              GUARD

          Excuse me?

Simon looks up at the guard

                              SIMON

          Oh, shit, man, I'm sorry. I didn't know
          it was the cops.

The guard looks up to his PARTNER behind the wheel and
shakes his head quickly, then takes his hand off his
holster.

                              GUARD

          Do you need any help?

                              SIMON

          No, thanks, bro, it's just the hose, I
          almost got it. Damn thing comes off alla
          time. It's the dang clamp that holds the
          hose to the...

Simon rambles as he looks under the car and then over
into it again. He gets on the ground under the car,
and while he is moving, his foot kicks the jack out of
place, the car teeters for a moment, and then

                              SIMON

          Holy...

From the angle that the guards are looking, the car
seems to fall on Simon. He wails and twitches.

                              GUARD

          Bill! Get out here.

He rushes over to where Simon lies on the ground
moaning, the driver opens his door and starts to get
out, but then reaches in for the radio.

> DRIVER

Hang on, I gotta...

Before he can say anything, Thack comes out from his hiding place and cracks his rifle butt on the back of the driver's head, and the man falls.

> THACK

Nighty night, dude.

The first guard reaches Simon. Jim is up in the back seat. He shoves the barrel of a shotgun through the back window pointed at the back of the guard's head.

> JIM

Freeze. Drop the piece.

The guard stops dead and then slowly takes out his gun and drops it. Simon gets up and picks up the guard's gun. Jim grabs a black duffel bag and then steps out of the car.

> JIM

Good boy.

Jim takes the guard back to the armored truck, making sure the guard is facing away, holding the shotgun to his head the whole time.

> JIM

Open it. Don't make me ask twice, Superman.

Simon is still by the car, watching the alley opening, he keeps looking at his watch.

> SIMON

Let's go guys.

> THACK

(under his breath) Shut the fuck up.

The guard opens the back doors of the truck and is knocked out by Jim, who then gets in the truck and starts to stuff money bags into his own duffel bag.

Thack comes around to the back to help when the side door to the jewelry store opens and a MAN pokes his head out. Then he shouts back over his shoulder.

MAN

> ...for a cigarette. Hey, the truck's
> stopped in the alley.

He starts to come out into the alley, laughing.

> What's going on, guys, huh? Holdup? Ha
> ha.

Thack is startled by the man and fires his shotgun at almost point blank range, hitting the steel door and knocking the man back into the doorway.

Simon and Jim both turn toward the sounds.

SIMON

> Holy shit on a wafer.

JIM

> What the Hell.

THACK

> Let's go Jimbo, go go go.

Simon starts toward Thack but is stopped when he hears screeching tires at the alley's mouth, it is Janie in another car.

SIMON

> Let's get the hell out.

THACK

> A little more, man. Still on schedule.

Another figure moves inside the store's side door. Thack fires in that direction, the figure retreats. The store's alarm sounds.

INT — JANIE'S CAR — SAME TIME

She sees the armored car driver getting up and pulling the shotgun out of the cab.

JANIE

> Thack! Look out, the driver.

Thack sticks his head around the side of the truck and pulls it back just as the driver gets off a shot. Thack sticks his shotgun around the corner and fires, then looks under the truck and sees the guard fall.

THACK

> Move, Jimbo.

                              JIM

          Done.

He jumps out from the back of the truck. He and Thack
run up toward Janie's car.

                              JANIE

          Hurry!

Janie revs the engine. Thack trips on the jack stand
and takes a moment to get going again.

Jim throws the bag of loot in ahead of them and then
jumps into the car, Thack gets in and yells to Simon.

                              THACK

          Get in!

                              SIMON

          What are you doing?

                              THACK

          Just shut the hell up and get in,
          dumbass.

Simon sprints to the car and jumps in as the it peals
out into the street.

                              THACK

          Janie, floor it! Jimbo?

                              JIM

          I don't see nobody.

                              THACK

          Yeah man! Haul ass, Bonnie, we got it.

                              JANIE

          Damn, baby.

Jim sees a patrol car round the corner behind them. It
stops momentarily as an officer gets out and runs to the
alley. The cruiser speeds after Thack's car.

                              JIM

          Uh oh. We got company, one car. Must
          have been in the area.

                              SIMON

          Damn it.

                    THACK

     Sorry. Had to improvise, man, somebody
     threw off the game.

Simon shoots a glance to Jim. Jim shakes his head and
shrugs.

                    JIM

     Guy from the store spooked us, we
     grabbed the deposit bags and ran. Just
     like you planned, man.

                    SIMON

     Yeah, just like.

Thack leans out and looks back toward the cop car.

                    THACK

     Gimmee, Jimbo

Jim pulls an automatic rifle out of a bag on the floor
and hands it over. Thack leans out the window and
starts shooting at the police car.

The windshield of the cruiser shatters and the car
crashes through a mailbox and a hydrant, then smashes
into a storefront.

                    THACK

     Burn rubber, Janie.

The car speeds around a corner.

EXT — CITY STREET — EVENING

Mike and Sharon walk slowly and wobbly up the street.

                    SHARON

     It's funny, cause for having such big
     feet, he's got a really little weenie.

She giggles drunkenly, Mike laughs.

                    MIKE

     What did you ever see in him?

                    SHARON

     I don't know, he used to be a little dif-
     ferent. Or maybe I was young and he was
     just really good at bullshitting.

                         MIKE

          I can't believe you would ever be fooled
          by a guy like him.

Sharon stops and looks at Mike, suddenly serious.

                         SHARON

          Nobody's born with it, Mike. We have to
          learn it from somewhere. He taught me
          how to watch out for people like him.

They resume walking.

                         SHARON

          But you know what, If I hadn't known him
          when I did, I wouldn't appreciate people
          like you.

                         MIKE

          Losers?

                         SHARON

          Knock it off. You're not a loser. You
          just let other people get the best of
          you too often. You never expect anyone
          to be truly as bad as they are.

                         MIKE

          So you're saying I'm dense?

                         SHARON

          You're a nice guy. And you know what
          they say about nice guys?

                         MIKE

          What?

They stop in front of an apartment building, She turns
to him.

                         SHARON

          Wanna come up?

She leans in and kisses him on the mouth, he doesn't
fight it too much. She leans back away from him.

                         MIKE

          (sincere) Maybe some other time, when
          we're both sober.

                    SHARON

    Good. I'm a really lousy lay when
    I'm drunk. Could you help me find my
    apartment. I left it near here.

                    MIKE

    Yeah, sure.

He helps her in the door.

EXT — ABANDONED FACTORY PARKING LOT — EVENING

Thack's car lurches to a stop. Janie and Thack jump
out cheering and laughing. Jim lumbers out and Simon
angrily exits.

                    SIMON

    Damn it, Thack, listen to me. This is a
    whole new game now.

                    JIM

    He's right, man. This ain't just simple
    robbery. We up to Murder maybe. Gonna
    have to disappear.

                    THACK

    Sure. Yeah. But we'll have to hang here
    for a while, till I can get in touch
    with our people. What'd we pull, Jimbo?

                    JIM

    Not Sure, couple hundred grand. Have to
    recount it inside.

                    JANIE

    Hear that, Clyde? Jackpot!

                    THACKERY

    No shit! We're in the money.

                    SIMON

    Thack, do you care at all?

                    THACK

    Comes with the territory. You think we
    could get away without shooting our
    whole lives?

Simon just stares at the ground, fuming.

                         SIMON

          If you'd ever stick to the...

                         THACK

          You're a damn broken record. Shit hap-
          pens, man! Plans change. Didn't think
          about that, did you smart guy?

Simon turns away shaking his head. Thack and Janie jump
back in the car.

                         THACK

             Go open that middle door, Jimbo, let's
             get inside and count our blessings!

Jim heads toward the large bay doors of the Factory and
pulls one open. Thack and Janie drive behind him into
the building. Simon walks in slowly as Jim pulls the
door closed.

EXT — INTERSTATE HIGHWAY — MORNING

Singing is heard as a large passenger van drives up
from the distance. As it gets close, the Granma's Ouija
Board sign on the side is visible. A road sign shows
Los Angeles is a few hours away.

INT — VAN INTERIOR — IMMEDIATELY FOLLOWING

Luther drives, Marla has shotgun, Sharon and Mike sit
in the middle seat. Colton, Tommy and Gil sit in back.
Bags are piled behind them.

Everyone except Luther sings along with a Doors tune at
the top of their lungs, and very off-key

                      EVERYBODY

             Yeah, I woke up this morning and I got
             myself a BEER. I'm going to the Road-
             house, I'm gonna have a RE-AL, GOOD TIME

Luther sucks on a joint and then passes it to Marla. He
holds it a second or two, then exhales.

                       LUTHER

             The way back, I pick the CD's.

INT — ABANDONED FACTORY STOREROOM — AFTERNOON

Thack, Jim, Janie and Simon sit on old chairs and
crates. The room is pretty dark and dusty, lit only
by some battery and fuel powered LANTERNS and the
scattered light from down the hall.

Two large STORAGE CELLS with steal mesh gates line a
wall. Some Fifty-five gallon DRUMS with warning labels
sit in one corner near the doorway.

                    JIM

    That's all I'm saying, man. This a whole
    new world of shit.

                    THACK

    And I keep telling you, Jimbo, I got
    connections, now. All I have to do is
    make a phone call and they come here and
    get us.

                    SIMON

    For free, right?

                    THACK

    No. Ten percent.

                    SIMON

    Jesus! That's over seventy grand.

                    THACK

    It ain't worth it to you?

                    SIMON

    You could have at least let us in on
    that before the job. You're just telling
    us now?!

                    JIM

    No big deal, Simon. We pulled more than
    we thought we would.

                    SIMON

    Where you gonna call these people from?
    No power, no phones here.

                    THACK

    So? I'll drive into town.

                    SIMON

    And you know for sure that the cops
    didn't get a make on our car, right?

                    JANIE

    What?

                         SIMON

          And you also know that they aren't just
          looking for crooks anymore, right?
          They're now looking for robbers who
          probably just killed a cop, security
          officer and innocent bystanders.

                         THACK

          Give me a break, man.

                         SIMON

          Yeah, no problem, Thack.

Jim and Janie look back and forth from Thack to Simon
and each other, nervous.

                         THACK

          You're pushing me, Foster.

                         SIMON

          Now you give me a break.

Thack glares at him, Simon holds his gaze. Thack
lightens up and starts to chuckle.

                         THACK

          Consider it given, bro. I messed up
          again. Sorry. Come on, what do you want
          me to say?

He offers a handshake, Simon just looks at him.

                         THACK

          Come on, help us get through this, then
          you can take off, no hard feelings, Okay?

                         JANIE

          Come on Sy, please.

There is a long a beat, finally he takes Thack's hand.

                         SIMON

          Yeah, whatever.

He shakes, the others heave a sigh of relief.

                         THACK

          Look, I'll go get us something to eat,
          you guys stay here and chill. Count the
          money again, whatever. Tonight I'll go

make the call, they'll pick us up, and
it's off to Mexico.

                    JIM

    Sure, Thack.

                    THACK

    Alright, cool. Janie, help me unload the
    car.

                    JANIE

    Sure, baby!

Thack and Janie, who grabs a lantern, leave. Jim and
Simon stare after them a moment.

                    SIMON

    Still trust him?

                    JIM

    Nope.

INT — THE HALLWAY — SAME TIME

Thack and Janie walk toward a large room at the end
of the hall. A little light creeps in through dirty,
broken windows. Thack whispers to Janie.

                    THACK

    You gotta stick with me, baby. Keep an
    eye on those two, don't let Simon turn
    Jimbo against us.

                    JANIE

    But I thought...

                    THACK

    Just do what I say, baby. Remember, this
    is for us.

They pass out of the hall and into the large room. They
are on the upper level of a production room.

Large, dusty machines stand in rows on the first floor
covered in layers of dust, debris and bird shit. Huge
spools of wiring and tubing are piled.

They climb down the metal staircase.

EXT — LA CITY STREET — AFTERNOON

The Ouija Board van pulls up to the curb in front of a
well-lit theater front. The marquee reads "THE ANGEL'S

THEATER" and beneath it, "Appearing this weekend
Granma's Ouija Board: Improv Comedy at it's best!"

                         MARLA

     Wow! Look at that.

The troupe piles out of the van stretching and
bitching, but excited. They look up at the marquee.

                         TOMMY

          My ass hurts!

                          GIL

          With an ass that size, you must be damn
          near in a coma.

                        SHARON

          Ooh! Look at that! Our name in lights!
          Oh, the Big Time. Stardom. Fame, for-
          tune! I'm wet.

                        COLTON

          I distinctly remember asking for top
          billing. I'm calling my agent.

                         MIKE

          Let him call you, they get one phone
          call.

They all take in the street and coolness of where they
are and why. Luther gets out of the van.

                        LUTHER

          Let's get the props and stuff inside.
          We're supposed to have a dressing room
          ready. Somebody find a local paper.

They start to unload.

INT — ANGELS THEATER INTERIOR — DAY

The troupe walks down the aisle toward the stage
carrying bags and large plastic bins. The stage is much
bigger than the one at Gypsy Cart, the theater seats
about seven hundred.

                         TOMMY

          Oh man, look at that! And look at all
          the seats!

                         SHARON

          Yeah. Now three times as many people can
          watch you fuck a goat onstage.

Tommy fakes wiping a tear.

                         TOMMY

          Mom would be so proud.

Colton jumps onto the stage as they pass by to go to
the dressing room, and addresses the "audience"

                         COLTON

          Thank you so much for coming tonight,
          I'm Colton, Colton Blanks, and I'd like
          to end my show with a tribute to The
          Mills Brothers.

He starts to sing "Glow Worm" as his friends boo him off
the stage.

                         COLTON

          Wow, listen to those acoustics.

He jumps back down and follows the troupe.

EXT — LA CITY STREET — EVENING

Thack walks warily down the street, his hands shoved
deep into his pockets. He rounds a corner and almost
runs right into a police car parked at the curb. He
balks, then turns and walks away quickly, catching
their attention.

                         COP ONE

          Let's check that out.

The cops follow as Thack ducks back around the corner.
They see a throng of people coming and going in front
of the theaters, bars and restaurants. They search for
Thack in the crowd but then meet up again.

                         COP ONE

          He's probably just drunk and stupid.

They head back toward their car.

INT — ANGELS THEATER LOBBY — EVENING

Thack looks over his shoulder as he nervously makes his
way into the back of the theater. We can hear laughter
and something in progress on stage.

                         THACK

          What the hell is this?

Thack pushes through the people standing with drinks
at the back of the show room. He slips into the mass,
still looking over his shoulder, and finally settles
himself, his attention is fixed on the stage.

Gil and Mike are on stage in the middle of a game.

                          GIL

          Right, good suggestions. We now present
          our scene of a bank robber, a ruptured
          uvula, of all things, and a runcible
          spoon.

Thack sees the audience laughing, and gets interested.
Mike walks off stage, then reenters and walks to Gil.

                          GIL

          Hi, may I help you?

                         MIKE

          Uh, yeah, does this bank have Free
          Checking?

                          GIL

          Yes, sir, it does. Thanks to that guy
          who shot up the place a few weeks ago,
          we've changed our policy.

He holds out his hand.

          Free pen?

This line gets a huge response, they go with it.

                         MIKE

          Oh, that was here, wasn't it?

                          GIL

          Yeah, good thing we read the papers in
          rehearsal.

                         MIKE

          Anyway, I need to open an account.

Sharon jumps in from the side with her fingers formed
into guns.

                        SHARON

          Awight thtickem' mup!

                    GIL

What did she say?

                    MIKE

I believe it was like "Lick a mop"

                    SHARON

Thticken mup!!

                    MIKE

Oh! "Stick 'em up!" Sounds like she has
a uvula problem.

                    GIL

What is a "uvula" anyway, I thought...

He points toward his crotch.

                    MIKE

No, no no, it's that little thing that
hangs in the back of your throat.

                    GIL

Damn, there goes half of my jokes.

                    SHARON

I thed Thticken mup! Thith ith a bank
robbewy.

She starts to fire her "gun"

                    SHARON

Bang bang bang bang

                    MIKE

Yow! What are we gonna do?

                    GIL

Hope she wastes all her ammo on the
walls, then we can rush her! Just like
the last guy.

                    SHARON

Click, click, Oopth.

Thack gets increasingly more angry as the sketch
progresses. He mumbles under his breath

                    THACK

Fuck you. I don't talk like that.

He has some trouble getting out of the area he is in,
but finally manages to squirm angrily out to the aisle.
He looks back to the performance. Marla has come on to
the stage

                         MARLA

         Never fear, I'll save you.

                          MIKE

         My hero!

                         MARLA

         No, not you, I mean her. I'm a surgeon.
         I can fix her uvula.

                          GIL

         Ooh, can we watch?

                         MARLA

         Pigs! Take that.

She swings at Mike and pops him right in the jaw. Mike
goes down, really hurt. The audience roars. He gets up
slowly, Gil covers for him

                          GIL

         Did you say "surgeon" or "sturgeon?" I
         think you ruptured his epiglottis.

The audience laughs. Thack works his way out of the
crowd and finds his way to the front door. He sees the
sign in the lobby advertising Granma's Ouija Board.

                         THACK

         You think you're funny?

He storms out into the street and looks up and down the
sidewalk, then heads off.

A line and a burst of laughter is heard as another
patron opens the door going in.

INT — FACTORY STORAGE ROOM — NIGHT

Janie, Jim and Simon re-pack bags on one of the old
desks they have cleared off.

                         JANIE

         Come on guys, don't you think you're be-
         ing a little unfair?

                    JIM

     Janie, I been with you guys for years.
     He's getting spooky.

                    SIMON

     And don't try to make it look like I'm
     just paranoid or anything, I saw you
     with that look on your face, too.

Janie thinks for awhile while she loads up a bag with
neat stacks of bills.

                    JANIE

     He's just excited, that's all. This was
     a big job.

                    SIMON

     No, when you're excited you wet your
     pants or get a stiffy. Thack may have
     killed a couple people.

Janie gets annoyed. She yanks the zipper closed on the
bag she's packing.

                    JANIE

     Look! If you can't handle it, Foster,
     then get the hell out. Now! Go ahead,
     take your share of the money and clear
     the fuck out.

                    JIM

     Janie...

                    JANIE

     You too, Jim. Thack has never done any-
     thing to hurt you or cheat you and now
     you're turning on him too. Here's the
     money, take what's yours and get out.

Simon and Jim just look at each other, unsure of what
to say.

                    JIM

     (calmly) Ok, Janie. But I think we need
     to talk to him first.

                    JANIE

     Are you stupid?

She drags the bags onto the floor and storms out of the room. Jim and Simon look uneasily at each other.

INT — THE ANGELS THEATER — NIGHT

Marla and Mike exit the stage on the same end, everybody else exits the opposite side. Marla nervously casts glances at a seething Mike. Colton is onstage.

> COLTON VO
>
> Ahh, bank robbers, you gotta love 'em. Anyhoo, we have one last game for you tonight...

The audience gives a collective "Awwww, no!"

Mike is holding his jaw, obviously in pain.

> MIKE
>
> Hey Marla, meet me back by the cooler for a sec, huh?

> MARLA
>
> Sure. Sure...

Marla is nervous as she hurries to catch up with him. Mike whirls suddenly and aims a finger sharply at Marla,

> MIKE
>
> I swear to fuckin' god... you pop anyone else on stage EVER again, I will knock every one of your fuckin' teeth out. DO YOU UNDERSTAND?

She nods weakly.

> MARLA
>
> Uh-huh

Mike sticks a finger in his mouth and pulls out a bloody TOOTH CHIP and flicks it across the room. Then he turns and goes to the cooler for water. He sloshes the water around in his mouth and groans in pain.

> MIKE
>
> God DAMNit.

He walks away as Marla just stands there. She makes a few glances to see if anyone else saw, shakes her head and leaves in the other direction.

EXT — ANGELS THEATER PARKING LOT — LATER

Thack smokes a cigarette and paces near the back

entrance. He is cursing and spitting. Marla storms out
the back door to the club and runs into Thack.

MARLA

What the...

THACK

Watch it, assho... oh, sorry.

He recognizes her.

Hey, aren't you in this, this comedy
show thing?

He gestures with his cig up at the theater

MARLA

Yeah, the improv troupe... Grandma's
Ouija Board

THACK

Yeah, that's it. I just saw your show.
Pretty funny.

MARLA

Thanks.

THACK

You look a little upset, there, honey.
Smoke?

He offers a cigarette, Marla shakes her head "no" and
produces a JOINT. Thack lights it for her and they walk
toward the parking lot.

Thack makes a few quick glances around. Marla takes a
huge toke and offers it to Thack, who declines.

THACK

I saw you in that gangster skit you guys
did. You were great.

MARLA

(laughs) Yeah? That wasn't a skit,
though. It was improv.

THACK

What?

MARLA

You know, we get ideas from the audience
and then we make up stuff as we go along.

> THACK
>
> Make it up as you go? I like that.

They stop near the troupe's van, Marla leans against it and takes a long drag on the joint. Thack glances around again quickly.

He sees the magnetic sign on the side

> From out of town huh?

Marla turns her back on Thack and looks at the van sign.

Thack's gaze nervously sweeps the parking lot, he flicks his cig butt away and moves quickly on Marla.

INT — ANGELS THEATER STAGE — SAME TIME

The audience roars and whistles as the cast takes the stage for their bows. Tommy is on the mic.

> TOMMY (VO)
>
> Thank you Los Angeles for coming to see us tonight, we are Granma's Ouija Board! Let's give it up for

As each player is announced they come front and center and do a little schtick, and then circle around to the back of the stage again.

> Mr. Gil "I beg your" Pardon; Stan "the Man" Luther; Mike "the Mechanic" Stefanik; Madam Sharon Macintire; Colton "shootin nothin' but" Blanks; The Mysterious Disappearing Marla Pierce;

Luther looks around as Marla's name is mentioned, then he glares at Mike, who just shrugs and laughs like it's part of the show.

> I'm Tommy "Boy" George. We are Granma's Ouija Board, we have one more show tomorrow night, tell your friends, tell your enemies. Goodnight!

The applause dies out, they exit the stage and a COMIC takes their place and starts to make announcements about the next show.

> COMIC (VO)
>
> Oh man, don't know if I will ever think about Vegemite and herd animals the same

way again. Give it up one more time for
Granma's Ouija Board, they've got one
more show tomorrow night. But hang out
with us for just a few more minutes,
please. We've got some great Stand-Up
coming to the stage next with

Granma makes its way backstage, Luther hurries over to
Mike, livid.

> LUTHER

Where's Marla?

> MIKE

Don't know, not my turn to baby sit.

> LUTHER

You and her took off after the bank thing
and no one's seen her since.

> MIKE

I asked her to kindly stop hurting
people onstage, and she had a fit and
took off.

> LUTHER

She completely missed the curtain.

> MIKE

Wish I could say the same about my jaw.

> LUTHER

Quit being such a pussy, Stefanik. Shit
like that happens in improv.

> MIKE

Then why does that happen in this
troupe?

> LUTHER

You don't like the way things happen?

> MIKE

No, I don't.

> LUTHER

There's the fucking door.

> MIKE

Ahhh, very good. You've been studying,

> Grasshopper, now, where is the ceiling,
> the ceiling?

The two stare at each other for a second or two. Luther boils. Mike just looks at Luther with an insincere grin.

> LUTHER
>
> No notes, get everybody in the van.

He turns to leave.

> MIKE
>
> Oh, we're taking the van?

> LUTHER
>
> What else are we gonna take?

> MIKE
>
> Well, you were leaving in a huff, so I thought we'd all pile into that.

Luther flips him off as he walks away.

> MIKE
>
> Thanks, no.

Mike shakes his head and turns, running into Tommy.

> TOMMY
>
> We doing notes?

Mike gets jittery, like a nervous little cartoon dog.

> MIKE
>
> We doin' notes? Huh? Huh? Are we? Can we go do notes, please, please? Huh, can we?!
>
> (Back to normal)
>
> No, we are not doing notes, get everyone out to the van.

> TOMMY
>
> Right.

He runs off calling out names of the troupe.

> Sharon, Gil, let's go! Marla?

> MIKE
>
> Spaz.

He turns and walks out the back door.

INT — ABANDONED FACTORY — NIGHT

Simon and Jim pace around.

> SIMON
>
> Man, what is taking him so long. Did he
> say where he was going?

> JIM
>
> Nah, just into the city. Had to meet
> with some people.

Jim takes out a cigarette and lights it.

> SIMON
>
> Take is easy with that shit.

He motions toward the barrels in one corner with the
warning label on them.

Janie enters from the hallway.

> JANIE
>
> Where is he?

The two men just shrug

EXT — ANGELS THEATER PARKING LOT — EVENING

Luther, Mike, Sharon, Colton and Gil meet at the van.
They are all on a rush from the great show.

> LUTHER
>
> Where the hell is she? Is Tommy back
> yet?

> GIL
>
> Here he comes.

Tommy comes jogging out the back door.

> GIL
>
> Tommy, you find her?

> TOMMY
>
> Nope.

> SHARON
>
> Shouldn't be hard to find her, then. How
> many opium joints can this city have?

                    MIKE

     Opium Joints? Do they still make those?

                    GIL

     Yeah, but they're called "dens" not
     joints.

                    SHARON

     Well, then that would make her a Den
     Mother.

                    MIKE

     Let's go SCOUT her out.

                    SHARON

     If WE BELLOW, she might hear us.

                    COLTON

     Ooh, do we get BROWNIE points if we find
     her?

Luther gets pissed

                    LUTHER

     Get in the van, if she ain't back in five
     minutes, she can find her own way back.

                    SHARON

     Eeew, it's always ugly when they eat
     their own.

Luther gets in behind the wheel, everyone else opens
the side doors, Tommy shouts and heads for the front
seat

                    TOMMY

     Shotgun!

He jumps in, as Sharon, Colton, Gil and Mike get in the
back.

Thack appears from out of nowhere and shoves a gun into
the back of Colton's head and pushes him into the van,
getting in behind him.

                    THACK

        I ain't got no shotgun, but I think
        this'll work.

Everybody freezes, Colton gasps. Luther at first doesn't
realize what is going on, he turns to see.

                    LUTHER

What the hell?

                    THACK

Drive, or you'll lose your cleaning
deposit on this rental.

                    LUTHER

Great.

He turns back around and starts the van. Colton finally
speaks.

                    COLTON

We were waiting for our friend, if she
finds we're not here.

                    THACK

I wouldn't worry about her. She couldn't
find a joke in a bag of assholes.

The statement weighs on them for a second.

                    SHARON

Oh my god.

                    MIKE

(to himself)

There goes our ticket sales.

The van pulls out of the parking lot and speeds down
the street.

INT — ABANDONED FACTORY — NIGHT

Jim, Simon and Janie stand just inside the loading area
bay doors. Jim and Janie smoke. Simon leans against
the wall with his arms folded. A car horn blasts, they
start at the sound.

                    SIMON

Thack?

                    JANIE

Doesn't sound like the car. Something
bigger.

                    SIMON

Jim!

He motions toward one side of the big bay doors, then
motions to the other

                              SIMON

          Janie!

Janie and Jim do as they are told, Simon pulls his gun
and approaches the bay door and peeks through a crack.

He sees the Granma's Ouija Board van pull up to the
doors and stop. Thack gets out, pointing his gun
inside.

                              THACK

          Janie! It's me, open up!

Simon turns his head.

                              SIMON

          Open up Jimbo, it's him. He's got some-
          one with him.

Thack sees the bay door opening, and he gets back in
the van. It pulls into the factory, and the door closes
behind it.

INT — STORAGE ROOM — evening

Jim pulls the steal mesh doors closed on one of the
storage cells, which is now filled with a bunch of
improv comics. He twists the toggle lock, pulls out the
key, then stands looking at the scared prisoners in
disbelief.

                              JANIE

          Thackery?

                              THACK

          Quiet, baby.

He brandishes his gun and approaches the cell with a
stupid grin on his face.

                              THACK

          Well, I suppose you're all wondering why
          I called you here tonight.

He laughs. Jim, Simon and Janie eye him uneasily, as
does the troupe.

                              THACK

          I saw your show tonight. It was pretty

lame. Especially the part about the bank robber.

                    SHARON

Oh... shit...

                     MIKE

What?

                    SHARON

It's him, the stupid guy who robbed that bank.

                      GIL

We're screwed

                     THACK

You guys need to make up for that crappy show.

              SIMON/MIKE/SHARON

What?

                     THACK

If you do, I'll forget about the other shit.

                    LUTHER

What other shit?

                    SIMON

Thack, what the hell is this?

                      JIM

I gotta go with Sy on this one, bro, you're tripping.

                    COLTON

Oh, this is encouraging, even the other bad guys think this is messed up.

                     THACK

Everybody shut up. Just shut up.

Janie pulls Thack aside

                    JANIE

Thackery, why are you doing this, baby?

                    THACK

     Because, Bonnie, I'm tired of being
     treated like some kind of idiot. It's
     bad enough I gotta take crap from Foster
     and Jimbo,

He gets Louder, turns toward the cage

                    THACK

     but tonight I'm dodging cops and I see
     these fuckers making fun of me, on a
     stage in front of the whole city.

He walks over to the mesh door and stares at Gil.

                    THACK

     If I'm so fucking stupid, then how come
     I've got half a million dollars in them
     bags over there, huh?

Thack motions to the bags under the table. The comics
all shoot a glance at the money.

                    THACK

     Do you have five hundred thousand
     dollars? Do you, funny man?

                    GIL

     No.

                    THACK

     How much do you have?

                    GIL

     I don't know. Probably twenty bucks.

Thack puts out his hand.

                    THACK

     Gimmee.

Gil fumbles through his pockets and produces a wadded
up twenty and slips it through the mesh. Thack grabs
it and waves it in front of Gil's face.

                    THACK

     Who's stupid now? Huh? Huh?

                    GIL

     I guess I am.

                    THACK

    Yeah.

He turns and walks back toward Janie.

                    THACK

    You got one more chance to make me
    laugh. Your friend said people tell you
    what to say.

                    TOMMY

    Well, not exactly. We do improv scenes
    with suggestions from the audience. You
    see, improv is different from stand up
    comedy in that...

                    THACK

    Shut up.

                    SIMON

    Seriously Thack...

                    THACK

    Zip it. We got plenty of time to kill.
    (a beat) Now, I need to get some sleep.
    Jimbo, Simon, keep your eye on them.
    They move, shoot them.

                    SIMON

    What are they going to attack us with,
    observational humor? "hey, what's up
    with that" jokes?

Thack and Janie take a battery-operated lamp and leave
the room.

Jim and Simon exchange glances. Jim shrugs and sits in
a chair facing the cage. Simon leans against a desk and
stares speechless at the guests.

INT — HOSTAGE ROOM — MORNING

Simon changes the batteries in a lamp near the cage.
Mike and Sharon sit with their backs against the wall
of the cell near the gate.

                    MIKE

    Hey, what's going on, man?

                    SIMON

    Talking to the wrong person, Jack.

                         MIKE

          My name's Mike. This is Sharon.

                        SHARON

          Hi.

Simon doesn't answer at first. He is tired. Finally he
looks up.

                         SIMON

          Hey.

                        SHARON

          Hey.

                         SIMON

          So, you just make everything up, no
          script? No plan?

                         MIKE

          Yup.

                         SIMON

          Must be fun. (a beat) You guys can't be
          very good though.

                         MIKE

          Why's that?

                         SIMON

          Well, your timing sucks.

                        SHARON

          Amen. What's with your friend?

                         SIMON

          Too tired to give the whole soap opera,
          but suffice it to say he's nuts.

They are surprised by a noise, it's Tommy, snoring and
re-adjusting his "bedding" on the floor.

The rest of the cast sleeps leaning against the walls
or each other.

Simon takes a quick look over at Jim, who sleeps in his
chair.

                         SIMON

          We don't give a shit about you guys, we

just wanted to do our thing and get the
hell out.

                    MIKE

Then let us go, man.

                    SIMON

Don't think I can do that.

                    SHARON

Why not?

                    SIMON

Common sense. You've seen us, you have
a good idea of who we are. And you know
what we got.

                    MIKE

Come on, we don't care. We're not even
from here. That guy is gonna kill us.

                    SIMON

Naw, we just need time to split.

Simon doesn't quite believe what he just said, and it
shows on his face.

                    SHARON

He is, isn't he?

                    SIMON

I don't know. I'm tired.

He sets the lantern down and gets to his feet and
lumbers back to the desk and sits behind it. Jim stirs
at the noise.

                    JIM

Hey bro, what up?

                    SIMON

S.O.S., man. Same Old Shit.

                    JIM

What time is it?

Simon looks at his watch.

                    SIMON

Half past "too fuckin late," Jimbo.

                          JIM

          (eyes the prisoners) I hear ya.

Mike continues to watch Simon, whispers to Sharon.

                         MIKE

          There's something about him I don't
          like.

                        SHARON

          He's seems okay, except for the fact
          that he looks just like Stan with long
          hair and a beard.

                         MIKE

          That's it. Poor bastard.

Stan stirs from his slumber and sits up. He looks
around and his gaze settles on Mike.

                        LUTHER

          Still here.

                         MIKE

          Yeah, man, we're still in jail.

                        LUTHER

          No, I meant you're still here.

Stan rolls over and shuts his eyes. Mike and Sharon
look at each other and manage weak smiles. They lean
their heads back and try to sleep.

INT — STORE ROOM — LATER

Indirect light filters in from the production room.
Simon and Jim both sleep at the desk.

Janie enters the room with a bag of fast food. She sets
it on the desk and kicks Simon's foot.

                        JANIE

          Sy, Jim, get up.

Simon stirs and looks up, then Jim awakens.

                        SIMON

          What's up, Janie?

                        JANIE

          Breakfast. Thack's out using the can,
          he's on his way up.

                         JIM

         Tell me he's forgotten about this.

Janie doesn't look at them, she takes food out of the
bag and sets it on the table.

                        SIMON

         We have to let them go, Janie.

                        JANIE

         I know that. Damn it, I know that.

Thack's voice, coming from the doorway, startles her.

                        THACK

         Know what, baby?

She turns and sees Thack in the doorway. He looks like
hell, dark circles under his eyes, messy hair, rumpled
clothes. A cigarette hangs from his mouth.

                        SIMON

         I was just bitching about the coffee
         being cold, Thack.

                        THACK

         Sounds like you, Foster. You guys eat,
         we need to get this show on the road.

He shuffles into the room and grabs a breakfast
sandwich. He has a gun in both the front and back
of his belt.

                         JIM

         What show, bro?

                        THACK

         Don't pull that crap on me, Jimbo. I
         meant what I said.

He walks over to the cage and bangs on the gate.

         These bastards are gonna pay.

The prisoners stir, stretch and get to their feet
slowly.

                       COLTON

         Oh, so this wasn't just a good dream.

                        GIL

         I smell coffee.

                    THACK

        Ain't for you, funnyman. I got something
        else in mind for you.

                    LUTHER

        You found a new playmate, Gilbert. Take
        him home to meet the wife, she'll like
        him. Nice change from you, I'll bet?

                    MIKE

        Don't start up so early, Stan.

                    LUTHER

        Mr. Non-Committal. Probably wouldn't
        even care, would you?

                    GIL

        Shut your fucking mouth, you heaping
        pile of shit.

The others all the sudden are wide awake, their eyes
are wide open and staring. Sharon and Gil look at each
other in astonishment.

Luther actually is taken aback by this remark, but
quickly regroups.

                    LUTHER

        Whoa, pussy-whipped boy grew a spine
        last night and...

Before Luther can say another word, Gil smashes his fist
into Luther's mouth, sending him reeling backward.

                    COLTON

DAAAAAAAA-YUM!

                    THACK

        Fight. Fight.

Simon, Jim and Janie look up and rush to the gate.

                    SIMON

        What's going on?

                    MIKE

        Gil finally showed how he feels about
        Stan.

Luther is on his feet, leaning against the wall and
wiping blood from his lip with the back of his hand.

                    LUTHER

    You're gonna wish you hadn't done that
    just now.

                     GIL

    I already wish I hadn't done it just
    now. I wish I had done it two years ago.

                    THACK

    Oooh, tough guy.

Gil wheels on Thack.

                     GIL

    Let's get this shit-show on the road.

                    THACK

    Easy there. Big fella. There's time. I
    need to finish my sandwich first.

                    SIMON

    Quit messing with him, Thack.

                    THACK

    Why don't you shut your yapper? You
    don't have people calling you an idiot
    all the time.

                     GIL

    God damn it, buddy, get over it. It was
    at best six hundred people. Exactly what
    the hell is your problem. We're comics.
    We read shit in the paper and make fun
    of it, we have nothing against you per-
    sonally, we go for laughs. If we stepped
    on your toes, I'm sorry, but get on with
    your life you crazy little fuckin' dick.

                    JANIE

    (barely audible) Oh shit.

Thack stares at Gil who waits for some kind of reply;
he is sweating. Thack finally speaks.

                    THACK

    Get him out here. Jimbo, gimmee the key.

                     JIM

    Simon has it.

                    THACK

          Foster! Open this friggin' box up and
          get him out here, and these guys, too.

He indicates Colton and Luther.

          Bring them out, bring them out.

Simon fumbles in his pocket for the key, Luther smiles
evilly. Mike grabs Gil's arm.

                    MIKE

          You can do it, man.

                    GIL

          He doesn't care.

Simon opens the gate and lets Gil, Luther and Colton
out, then swings the door shut. He looks up at Mike as
he fiddles with the lock

                    SIMON

          Stay away from the fucking door.

His eyes dart downward, Mike and Sharon follow his gaze
and see that he is NOT locking the door.

                    MIKE

          Kiss my ass.

Sharon mouths the words "thank you"

                    COLTON

          Why do I get the feeling working for
          this guy is gonna make Luther look like
          Mother Theresa?

The three stand in front of the gate facing Thack.

                    THACK

          Now I want to see some funny shit. Think
          you can handle the pressure, funnyman?

Gil just stares at Thack and says nothing.

                    THACK

          Come on, do something.

                    COLTON

          Uh... we need... input from you guys so
          we know what to do the scene about.

                    LUTHER

    Jesus, just fucking shoot me right now.
    Come on, right here.

He points to his own forehead.

                    THACK

    What's your problem, bro, no faith in
    your peers?

                    LUTHER

    Peers, my ass. I've been working with
    these losers for three years, and any
    time there's even the slightest pres-
    sure, they freeze up.

                    MIKE

    Jesus, Luther, shut up.

                    LUTHER

    You shut up, Stefanik.

                    SHARON

    Stan, for once in your life can give
    it a fuckin' rest?

Luther turns towards those in the cage.

                    LUTHER

    What'samatter, crybabies? You all scared
    because you know you suck, only this
    time the audience ain't just walking out
    on you, they want to kill you.

The members of the troupe all start to berate Luther,
who barks back at them.

Thack fires two rounds into the ceiling.

                    THACK

    Shut up! (after it quiets) This is
    getting better and better. I know how
    you feel, bro.

He glares at Jim and Simon, walks over to Luther.

                    THACK

    I like you, man. You don't put up
    with shit from these jealous bastards.
    Alright, you need "input" from us? What
    do you need?

Luther, Gil and Colton look at each other. Luther
throws up his hands and chuckles.

> LUTHER
>
> Alright, I'll play along, what the hell?
> A geographical location.

> THACK
>
> Simon.

> SIMON
>
> What?

> THACK
>
> Give the man a location.

> SIMON
>
> Give me a fucking break.

> THACK
>
> Now!

> SIMON
>
> ...San Francisco?

> LUTHER
>
> Okay, good, now we need an occupation.

> THACK
>
> Jimbo.

> JIM
>
> I don't know. I'm no good at this shit,
> man.

> THACK
>
> How fucking hard is it to come up with
> an occupation, Jimbo? We worked fifteen
> jobs together; framing houses, trash
> collector, Give the man a stinkin' job.

> JIM
>
> Christ. Okay, a... a grocer.

Janie and Simon and Thack all do a take at Jim, who
just shrugs.

> LUTHER
>
> Okay, San Francisco, a grocer, and now a
> major historical event.

                    THACK

That's yours baby.

                    JANIE

The... the... World War Two.

                    LUTHER

Alright! Here is our scene of a grocer
in San Francisco during World War Two.

He turns to Gil and Colton and speaks low.

                    LUTHER

What do you say guys, want to show what
you're made of? I don't want to die. How
about you, Blanks?

                    COLTON

Hell no.

                    LUTHER

Up to you, Gil.

Gil stares at Luther for a second, then glares at
Thack.

                    GIL

Let's do it.

                    LUTHER

Good boy. See if you can keep up.

Luther moves a little to the side. Gil and Colton balk
at first, then do likewise. Luther walks toward them and
surveys the room.

                    LUTHER

Boy do I hate Japs. Always looking for
weird vegetables at my humble American
grocery store. We should lock them up
in prison camps. Let's go up to Grant
Avenue and round 'em all up.

                    GIL

That's China town.

                    LUTHER

Chin-ese, Japan-ese what's the
difference. They're all ese-ian.

                              GIL

          Well, if China had made the planes that
          attacked Pearl Harbor, they would've
          fallen apart before they reached the
          island.

Thack laughs as he backs up and sits on a desk. Simon,
Janie and Jim stand nearby, casting uneasy glances back
and forth.

                             THACK

          Yeah, no shit, damn Chinese make some
          crap, man.

Mike, Sharon and Tommy watch the scene, sweating. Tommy
is on the verge of crying.

                             TOMMY

          I can't do this, Mike. I can't do this.

                             MIKE

          Just think of it as our regular drunk-
          en-college-student Friday nights.

                             SHARON

          Yeah, just drunken college students with
          guns.

Mike shoots her a look.

          Sorry.

                              GIL

          AAAAAANY-way... I'm here to pick up a
          grocery order for my boss.

Colton rushes in "the door," upset, perfect posture.

                             COLTON

          Fernwick, why are you taking so long,
          my wife needs those groceries for her
          War Bond party this afternoon!

                              GIL

          So sorry, Mr. Yamaguchi, I got caught up
          with

                             LUTHER

          YAMAGUCHI?! You're Japanese?!

Colton strikes a Superman pose.

Colton

Japanese... AMERICAN. I'll pay you
triple for that Bok-Choi order!

Luther

SOLD! (they "exchange money. To Gil) But
you... you filthy Jap sympathyzer!

He grabs Gil in a headlock and mimes pounding his face.

LUTHER

We've been doing without stuff, rationing
gas and chocolate... panty hose. I have
to piss on my Victory Garden because
water's short, and you buy groceries for
the yellow hord?

GIL

Again, that's Chin... wait, you wear
pantyhose?

COLTON

(to Luther) A transvesite?! I will NOT
eat produce from an abomination!

THACK

This Jap guy is hysterical!

LUTHER

What are you gonna do about it, big boy?

Luther makes a slight eye-shift toward Thack. Colton
picks up on it.

COLTON

Tora Tora Tora!

Colton rushes in on Luther, who steps aside, grabs
Colton's arm and sling-shots him dircetly at Thack.

LUTHER

Look out — Kamikaze!

Colton comes in hot, Thack has no time to react. Colton
plows into him, and in turn knocks Janie off her feet.

THACK

Hey, what the fuuu

Luther wheels on Gil and the other comics.

                    LUTHER

        TAG - you're it!

Luther dives at Jim and knocks him over, pummeling him.

Gil makes a charge for Simon and the two go against a
wall before Simon can react.

Thack scrambles to get to his feet and tries to get his
gun out. Janie wrestles with Colton.

                    LUTHER

        Let's get 'em. Go go GO.

Gil and Colton fight like crazy. Luther kicks Jim in the
crotch hard and Jim goes down.

Colton does a pretty good job of keeping Thack and
Janie occupied.

Gil has trouble with Simon, and finally gets thrown
between Thack and Luther.

                    Luther

            Christ, Gil, do I have to do everything
            myself?

Luther grabs Gil by the arm and hauls him to his feet.
Then he grabs one of the duffel bags full of money,
shoves Gil forward toward Thack and Simon and splits
for the door.

Thack gets off a wild shot and hits Gil, who drops.

Colton stands wide eyed. The rest of the troupe gasps
in horror, Tommy is sobbing.

                    TOMMY

        Oh my god.

                    SHARON

        Oh crap, Gil?

INT — HALLWAY — SAME TIME

Luther is on his way down the hall at top speed, he
glances over his shoulder and smirks.

                    LUTHER

            Usually we just cue lights at the end of
            a scene, but that'll work.

INT — STORE ROOM — SAME TIME

Colton looks up from Gil and glares at Thack. A beat
passes and then he charges full tilt.

                    JANIE

          Look out!

Colton plows into Thack and the two go sprawling to
the floor. Colton is on top for a few seconds, pounding
away.

Janie tries to pull Colton off and whacks him with the
butt of her gun. Colton staggers back into the mesh
door of the cell, hard.

Sharon, suddenly remembering, grabs the gate and gives
it a little push, it opens about an inch or so.

                    SHARON

          FUCK! Mike, the gate.

Mike and Tommy look at the door and then out at the
mayhem, then to Sharon.

                    MIKE

          Nice callback!

They charge forward and crash into the gate, which flies
open and hits Simon, knocking him over again.

                    MIKE

          Tommy, go after that bastard.

Mike shoots a finger toward the hallway as he goes for
Jim.

Sharon helps Colton up and goes after Thack.

                    THACK

          Janie, he got the money.

Thack empties his gun at the doorway, Tommy covers his
head with his arms and cringes as he runs out. All of
the bullets hit the walls or the drums of toxic liquid,
whose contents gush out onto the floor.

Sharon punches Thack in the face and knocks him back
against the wall.

Jim rushes Mike and they go headlong into the steal
mesh of the other cell.

Janie grabs a shotgun from the duffel bag and waves it
in Sharon's direction.

                         JANIE

          Stop it! Stop it!

Simon and Colton are in a corner, Simon overpowers
Colton and sends him to the floor. Janie aims waveringly
at Sharon, Simon sees her finger go for the trigger.

                         SIMON

          Janie, don't.

He dives at Janie and hits her arm just as she pulls
the trigger. The shot goes wild, hitting Jim, throwing
him back against the drums. He knocks an oil lantern
to the ground and falls.

The liquid ignites and flames start to spread.

Janie drops the gun.

                         JANIE

          Jim? Oh no.

Simon grabs Janie's arm and pushes her toward the
doorway.

                         SIMON

          Get out of here, Janie, go.

Janie doesn't budge

                         JANIE

          I can't leave him, Simon.

Simon looks over at Sharon who has backed away from
Thackery. Thack is getting up and has his gun out.

                         SIMON

          You too, get the hell out of here,
          quick.

Mike runs to grab Gil, who is trying to get to his
feet. Sharon helps Colton up and looks at Simon.

                         SHARON

          What about you?

                         SIMON

          I'm okay. I do this all the time.

Sharon balks for just a second, Thack gets his bearings
and sees people heading for the door.

                    THACK

     What are you doing, Foster? They're
     getting away.

Thack points his guns, Simon charges in at him. Janie
goes after Simon.

                    SIMON

     Get out now.

Sharon, Mike and Colton bolt out the doorway through
the quickly growing flames and charge down the hallway.

INT — PRODUCTION ROOM — SAME TIME

Tommy sees the staircase and scrambles for it,
disappearing over the side. He sees Luther disappear
around a corner at the bottom.

                    TOMMY

     Stan, wait for me.

INT — STORE ROOM — SAME TIME

Simon, Janie and Thack wrestle as the room is engulfed
in flames. Two shots are heard and they fall to the
floor.

INT — HALLWAY — SAME TIME

Mike, Sharon, Colton and Gil stop at the top of the
stairs. They hear the gunfire and look back as the flames
and smoke starts to flare out into the hallway.

                    MIKE

     God damn, this is shaping up into the
     gig from Hell.

                    SHARON

     We have to get Gil out of here fast, he
     losing a lot of blood.

Mike looks back at the flames and Thack and Janie who
have just emerged from the room. They turn back to
start down the stairs and see some movement at the
other side of the room.

                    SHARON

     There's Tommy! I think Luther's ahead
     of him!

Sharon and Mike start to move Gil down the stairs.

                         MIKE

          Crazy people in da house. Colton, cover
          our backs.

                         COLTON

          Yeah, sure, man.

They head down the stairs and into another room just as
Janie and Thack look down from above.

                         JANIE

          We lost them!

                         THACK

          No we didn't. That's a dead end,
          literally.

Thack and Janie move down the stairs and head after
Mike and Sharon. Suddenly a huge explosion rocks the
building, knocking them down.

Mike, Sharon, Colton and Gil charge from their room
past Thack and Janie.

The production room quickly fills with smoke and flame.

INT — ANOTHER ROOM — SAME TIME

The room is filled with ladders, pipes, piles of chains
and the like. Tommy charges in one door, he sees Luther
trying to open a door at the other end.

                         LUTHER

          Tommy! Help me with this door I think it
          leads outside. C'mon, man, we'll split
          the cash.

Tommy looks back and sees flames engulfing the Factory
past the doors he just came through. He rushes to
Luther. They try to force the door open.

Tommy grabs a pipe and starts to pry at the small
opening they have made, Luther wrenches the door open.

                         LUTHER

          Thanks, Tommy, you always were a team
          player.

Luther's sentence is cut short by the pipe hitting his
head. He crumbles to the floor. Tommy leans over him,
scared and angry, and grabs the duffel bag.

                         TOMMY

>   I may be a wishy-washy little coward,
>   Luther, but I sure as hell ain't stupid.

Tommy drops the pipe on Luther's legs and runs through the door and out into the huge loading area where the vehicles are parked.

Sharon and Mike rush into the room and see the door wide open and hear the van start up. There is no sign of Luther.

                        MIKE

>   I hope that's Tommy and not Stan. Sha-
>   ron, Colton, get Gil out to the van,
>   I'll hold them off.

                        SHARON

>   Oh, enough macho shit for one day, Mike.

                        MIKE

>   You want to stay and hold them off?

                        SHARON

>   Nice knowing you.

She heads out the door, stops and comes back to Mike and kisses him.

                        SHARON

>   I will be very sober when this is all
>   over, come back alive.

She heads out with Colton and Gil.

Mike goes back to the door they came in and sees Thack and Janie running for the room. He looks around to find a weapon, but before he can, the outside door slams shut.

Standing against the wall is Luther, bleeding from his head, one eye swollen shut, the pipe in his hand.

                        LUTHER

>   Looking for this, Mike?

                        MIKE

>   Nice shiner.

There is a commotion at the far end of the room and another door flies open, smashed by a desk that is pushed through it.

A second later Simon appears, staggering. He holds
a gun and has one hand holding some wadded up cloth
against his ribs.

He stumbles into the room and tries to point his gun in
the direction of Luther.

Thack and Janie enter from the same door that Mike did.
They see the situation. Thack smiles.

                    THACK

        Well, well, well. Looks like I'm gonna
        get what I want after all.

Mike looks at Luther then to Thack and Janie and then
to Simon. They have no idea what to do.

Another explosion rocks the building. Everyone in the
room staggers as debris falls from the ceiling, a few
burning beams fall in the middle.

EXT — ABANDONED FACTORY PARKING LOT — SAME TIME

The factory is quickly being engulfed by flames and
smoke. A third explosion sends debris flying into the
parking lot.

We hear gunshots and then the Ouija Board van plows
through the bay doors. A few figures run from the
factory just as it collapses.

INT — FOOLS COURT OFFICE — DAY

SUPERSCRIPT — "TWO MONTHS LATER"

The door opens and Mike exits followed by Tarry O'Doul.

                    MIKE

        Jesus Christ, you're all alike!

                    TARRY

        Oh, hey now, son, that hurts. I'll get
        those papers working.

                    MIKE

        Thanks, Tarry.

                    TARRY

        Thank you, Mike. I'm looking forward to
        a good season!

                    MIKE

        Yeah, me too.

As Mike walks down the hall and into the daylight of
the lobby, applause and laughter is heard. It gets
Louder, and the light gets brighter until it washes out
the whole scene.

As the light fades again, the main stage of Fool's
Court is seen. Spotlights play wildly across the stage,
theme music plays. Tommy stands to one side of the
stage, he has a mic.

                         TOMMY

            Thank you ladies and gentlemen! We are
            Granma's Ouija Board! You've been a
            great audience! Now let's give it up
            one more time for Mike "the Mechanic"
            Stefanik, "Madame" Sharon Macintire,
            "Breakfast at" Tiffany Carson, Mel "Lit-
            tle Jack" Horner, Andrea "Dorea" Hoffman
            and Stanley "The Manly" Lutheeeeer...

The cast takes the stage one at a time as their names
are called, waving and mugging, taking their places.

As Luther's name is called, he charges onstage waving
and high-fiving the other members. Mike waves him on.

INT — BURNING FACTORY — TWO MONTHS EARLIER

Luther, Mike, Simon, Thack and Janie stand in the
burning room looking at each other for a few seconds,
suddenly Luther rushes at Mike and they tumble away
onto the floor.

Thack keeps his gun aimed at Sharon, Simon lumbers
toward Thack, gun raised, he is met half way by Janie
who grapples with him.

                         JANIE

            Run, Baby!

A shot rings out and Janie falls to the floor. Thack is
crazy with rage he fires at Simon. One rips into Simon's
shoulder, another hits his leg and he falls, dropping
his gun.

Thack turns to shoot Mike, but is clobbered by a length
of pipe wielded by Luther. He drops his gun. A chunk of
debris falls between them.

Mike, Thack, and Luther all rush for guns. Luther and
Mike stand triumphant with guns aimed at Simon and
Thack.

Thack goes for the gun in the back of his belt, Luther
shoots him twice in the chest and he falls.

Mike looks toward Simon, then to the door. When he
looks back, Luther has his gun pointed right at Mike.

> LUTHER
>
> What are you waiting for, crybaby?
> There's the fucking door.

He SQUEEZES the TRIGGER rapidly a number of times, we
hear clicks. His evil grin turns to a frown. A beat,
and then a goofy smile and laugh escape his face.

> LUTHER
>
> Good thing you have no balls, or I'd be
> pretty scared right about...

A burning beam drops and crushes Luther. Mike backs
away.

> MIKE
>
> Fantastic timing.

He becomes aware of Simon, wavering on his feet. Mike
rushes to Simon and helps him out of the room as the
ceiling collapses.

In the loading area, Mike and Simon see the van nosing
toward the loading dock doors. Sharon is outside the
van and waves to Mike.

Sharon, Mike and Simon are just behind the van as it
crashes the doors, and they make it out just as the
whole building collapses.

INT — SHARON'S APARTMENT — DAY

Sharon sits on the couch. Mike stands behind her, his
arm in a sling, and they watch the news on TV.

> NEWSCASTER VO
>
> ... Killed in the blaze were members
> of the group of bank robbers that were
> also involved in a shootout with police
> that resulted in three deaths: Thackery
> Washburn, Janie Giller, Simon Foster and
> Jim Franklin. One member of the group of
> stand up comics is still missing, and
> she is believed to be dead, according to
> information obtained from survivors of
> the ordeal. None of the money has been

recovered, and it is thought to have
destroyed in the blaze as well. We now
go to Fire Chief Garrity of...

                    SHARON

Holy crap. You hear that?

                     MIKE

No shit. They called us stand-up comics.

                    SHARON

No, dumbass. He's dead.

Sharon and Mike look slowly to each other. Mike raises
an eyebrow.

INT — MAIN STAGE AT FOOL'S COURT — NIGHT

                     TOMMY

    ...and Stanley "The Manly" Lutheeeeer!
    I'm Tommy "Boy" George, Thank you and
    good night!

As Luther takes the stage, an ANKH tattoo is visible on
the back of his neck. It is Simon, clean shaven, short
hair. He is having a great time. The crowd loves him.

As the troupe forms a line to lock hands and take their
bows, we see Tarry in the wings, watching the action.

The crowd ROARS with whoops and cheers. Mike smiles and
looks offstage to where Tarry is in the wings. Tarry
smiles and spreads his arms wide as if to say "it's all
yours."

Mike puts the palms of his hands together and does a
shallow bow to him, then turns back to the audience.

                     TOMMY

    Stick around, we've got karaoke coming
    up, drink specials at the bar...

Tommy's voice trails off to almost inaudible, but we can
still HEAR laughter and applause as the camera pulls
way out through the back of the room.

We watch Mike and the cast play with the audience as we

FADE OUT

THE END